PSYCHOANALYTIC PSYCHOLOGY

Psychoanalytic Psychology

REUBEN FINE, Ph.D.

JASON ARONSON • NEW YORK

To

SIGMUND FREUD

WHO OPENED A WHOLE NEW WORLD

FOR MANKIND

That beauty is a thing beyond the grave,
That perfect, bright experience never falls
To nothingness, and time will dim the moon
Sooner than our full consummation here
In this odd life will tarnish or pass away.

D. H. Lawrence

CONTENTS

Preface

This book has arisen out of the effort to make psychology and psychoanalysis intelligible to a wide variety of students from many disciplines. An early systematization was attempted in lectures presented to joint meetings of the Department of Psychology of the University of Amsterdam and the Amsterdam Psychoanalytic Institute in 1961. Since then the ideas presented there have been broadened and deepened in many directions.

Two kinds of systematization are intertwined in the presentation. First of all there is a synthesis of the essentials of psychoanalysis. Naturally, such a synthesis begins with Freud, but it goes well beyond him, shoring up areas that he neglected, correcting mistakes that have since been pointed out, and exploring regions that he ignored or passed over too lightly.

In this sense the present work continues the synthesis contained in my previous one, *The Development of Freud's Thought*. It has not seemed either necessary or desirable to probe into the details of all the "schools" that have sprouted since Freud's death, inasmuch as careful examination shows that while various writers have taken issue with many of his positions, they have not actually really differed from his basic framework. A good case can be made for the thesis that the common division of psychoanalysis into schools is born out of personal rivalry rather than real intellectual differences of opinion. Accordingly the concentration throughout has been squarely on issues rather than persons. With the recognition that many first-class minds since Freud have made significant contributions to the field, a unification has been essayed which sifts out the important material from the unimportant or repetitious and integrates it into one coherent framework. Doctrinaire adherents of one point of view or another will no doubt be dissatisfied, but I hope that the book will be judged on its merits as a system of psychology, rather than on adherence to some outstanding figure.

The recognition is gradually taking hold that psychology, if it is to be more than an academic exercise, must embrace the totality of human functioning. But since the human being has been studied from so many different angles, such a position involves an integration of material from many disciplines that are sharply distinguished from one another. The need for such interdisciplinary integration is obvious. If the attempt is to be accorded any measure of success, it will show what many believe, that the artificial breakdown of the study of man into many different fields is indeed an arbitrary one, understandable for historical reasons, but not justified by scientific necessity. Experimental psychology, learning theory, psychoanalysis, cognitive psychology, clinical psychology, anthropology, sociology, history, and many other social sciences are all part of a broader field, the study of man.

Thus the second systematization attempted here is that of embracing all the sciences that study man under one umbrella, the dynamic image of man derived from psychoanalysis. It is important to remember that such a dynamic image is more of an inspiration than a specific set of hypotheses, a vision of what man is and what man might become. Even though such an image leaves much unanswered, or rather subject to further exploration, without it the various fields necessarily bog down in a deplorable kind of hyper-trivialization. The lack of a vision accounts for the huge amount of waste motion visible on the current scene, which the president of every major association feels called upon to condemn year after year.

A number of convictions dominate this work. First of all there is the conviction that value-free science is valueless science. Every thinker must state the point of view that dominates his research. The major position adopted here is that of a humanistic psychology, which insists that man can find happiness in accordance with an image that I call the analytic ideal. This analytic ideal has grown out of the most profound aspirations of Western man over the past two millennia. It embraces the best in the past, yet pushes well beyond it.

Second, there is the conviction that psychology, even though it is an empirical science, can no longer remain divorced from philosophy. The psychological activity of any human being is guided by his search for happiness in his terms. Any activity or experience studied by the psychologist must be evaluated in accordance with this dominating concern. Thus even the simplest perception of a color cannot be properly understood without an adequate explanation of why the individual is looking at the color. *A fortiori,* the study of more complex activities remains sterile unless the goals being pursued by the individual in the activity are also spelled out in considerable detail.

It is in this way that psychology can again build up a philosophical outlook. But the kind of philosophy that emerges is a radically new one, inasmuch as the philosophies of the past never had an adequate psychology available. As a result the past can be considered only a prologue. The philosophy-psychology derived from psychoanalysis supersedes the philosophies of the past.

In a work of such broad scope, necessarily many important areas will be treated all too briefly. My only excuse is that the book offers a systematic approach, not a final solution to all the problems raised. It is hoped that this approach, which summarizes useful past research, while omitting the numerous blind alleys, will lead to more meaningful research in the future.

My thanks go to Steno-Services and Mrs. Carole McQuinn for their careful typing of the manuscript; to my wife, Charlotte, for her selfless ministration to my needs, in spite of the narcissism forced on a writer; and to my publisher, Dr. Jason Aronson, for his constant encouragement and at times critical comments.

REUBEN FINE

New York
December 15, 1974

PSYCHOANALYTIC PSYCHOLOGY

CHAPTER 1

The Structure of Psychological Theory

THE DILEMMAS OF PSYCHOLOGY

To the proverbial visitor from Mars, psychology today looks like a mass of observations, many unrelated, in search of a theory. Since no such generally accepted theory exists, the field appears to be divided into groups of warring factions. The two major antagonists today are behaviorism, rebaptized learning theory, which still relies most heavily on experimentation, and psychoanalysis, which places its major trust in naturalistic observation. By and large behaviorism is pursued by academicians, while psychoanalysis is furthered by clinicians. The interaction of these groups still produces rather violent clashes.

Some have tried to resolve the dilemma by positing two systems of psychology, or two "scientific psychologies" (Cronbach, 1957). Such an approach has to be rejected; there can be only one scientific psychology. It is the thesis of this book that such a scientific psychology must be based on Freud's basic theory, in which the valid findings of learning theory and behaviorism can be incorporated, rather than the reverse, as is usually claimed.

The word "theory" comes from the Greek *theoria,* which means "imaginative vision." Such an imaginative vision of the human enterprise is provided most clearly by Freud and psychoanalysis, even though there is much in them that requires clarification and elaboration. It is because of this vision more than of any specific proposition

1

that Freud has been widely hailed as one of the seminal figures of the twentieth century.

Inasmuch as academic psychologists have been more concerned with scientific method than clinicians, who have rather naively accepted the status of second-class citizens, some comments about their image of science are in order. The prevailing position is that science is built up on the basis of experimental findings, which are then generalized into theories and laws. Procedurally the task is to set up hypotheses that are then submitted to experimental verification or falsification. To some extent this is useful; to some extent it is not. It is incorrectly stated that this is the procedure that built the physical sciences into their predominating position (Skinner, 1971).

ERRORS IN THE EXPERIMENTALIST POSITION

I have discussed this position in considerable detail and pointed to five errors inherent in it which prevent it from becoming an adequate scientific method for all psychology (Fine, 1958-1959). These errors are the following: (1) Experiment is overemphasized. The logical basis for experimentation in psychology is often lacking and many current experiments are meaningless. (2) The attempt to set up a completely hypothetico-deductive system, modeled on physics, has been made too soon. Hull's approach has been abandoned as premature. (3) As a result, the relation of theory to fact is often inadequately explored, with one of two consequences: either the theory remains pure speculation without a tie to the real world, or large quantities of valid data are labeled "irrelevant" or "unscientific" and ignored. (4) Another consequence of the incorrect role assigned to theory has been that content is relegated to a secondary role. Those who work in content are dubbed "applied psychologists" and told that their labors are "unscientific." Since any theory must involve an explanation of all data, this attitude toward content derives from a misunderstanding of science. (5) In terms of specific activities, the exaggerations of the behaviorist position have led to enormous waste motion and have excluded from scientific consideration for a considerable period of time many essential psychological phenomena, such as the dream and consciousness (Fine, 1970).

However, the proof of the pudding is in the eating. For the remainder of this work I shall concentrate on a more positive approach, to justify the claim that psychodynamics is the most suitable basis for a truly scientific psychology.

SOME GENERAL PRINCIPLES

Two preliminary points must be noted. Man (Saperstein and Gaines, 1973) must be looked upon as an active agent, who is always seeking something. In particular he is seeking happiness, as defined in his own terms. Second, from a methodological point of view, a clear distinction must be drawn between theory and experience (Sandler and Joffe, 1969). The raw data of psychology are experiences; hence psychology must explain all the varieties of human experience, past and present, here and there, in all areas of human functioning.

Any individual act can be expressed as the response of a person to a stimulus; in symbols $R = f(P,S)$. Inasmuch as considerable areas of the human being are not directly observable, intervening variables have to be assumed to explain the responses. To eliminate intervening variables, as Watson and some contemporary behaviorists have tried to do, is scientific gobbledygook. It also demonstrates an ignorance of the wide area that reasonable inference plays in even the most exact of all the physical sciences (Fine, 1960-1061).

The attempt to confine oneself to physiological measures within the organism has been made by many, including some psychoanalysts. Such a reduction of psychology to physiology has yielded only tenuous speculative hypotheses. Unless immediately relevant, physiological questions are omitted from this work.

DISSENT IN PSYCHOANALYSIS

Like psychology in general, psychoanalysis demonstrates many warring factions. There is no single source that can be pointed to as an authoritative statement of the psychoanalytic position. Freud's work was basic, and was codified by Fenichel in his *Psychoanalytic Theory of Neurosis*. But this book was first published in 1934, expanded in 1945. More than forty years have passed, and enormous changes have occurred. These have to be pulled together from many different sources.

It would be a mistake to assume a unanimity of opinion even among closely knit members of a single group, such as the American Psychoanalytic Association. The famous fiasco of the Fact-Finding Committee (Hamburg et al., 1967), which embraced the best minds of the society in the effort to set down the results of psychoanalysis, yet came up with a triviality, shows this more than any polemic.

Nor can much comfort be gained by sticking to the so-called schools of psychoanalysis (Fine, 1973). As the recent Freud-Jung letters show, even more clearly than anything else (1974), the element of personal rivalry within psychoanalysis is a bitter one, which has colored the literature with the grossest kinds of distortions. Such distortions unfortunately persist today.

The Freudian theoreticians who have made the best-known attempts to systematize psychoanalysis, such as Rapaport (1960) and Hartmann (1964), have tried to reduce the various propositions of psychoanalysis to an economic point of view. Apart from the fact that this has led to a metapsychological approach of a highly abstract and at times almost unintelligible character, such a basic stress on the economic point of view is erroneous. Freud himself was fond of it, true enough, but it is equally true that either he or his followers had to abandon every one of his economic formulations (Project, 1895; actual neurosis, 1890s; libido as a quantity, 1914; death instinct, 1920).

THE CENTRAL VISION OF PSYCHOANALYSIS

Yet Freud's central vision persists, and it is to this vision that we return over and over again. Central to psychoanalysis is (*a*) an imaginative view of what man is; (*b*) an imaginative view of what man might become; (*c*) an original conceptual framework with which to order and understand the data of human experience and behavior.

The view of what man is can best be described in terms of ego psychology, or the total personality structure. However, the notion that there is a special "school" of ego psychology, of which Hartmann is the chief exponent, must be rejected; all psychoanalysts since 1923 have been ego psychologists.

More useful is the expansion of Freud's metapsychological scheme, more properly called a "holopsychological" scheme, since it relates to the whole of psychology, and does not go beyond psychology. In this metapsychology, a mental act can be considered to be completely understood if it is approached from eight different points of view: (1) topographic, (2) genetic, (3) dynamic, (4) economic, (5) structural, (6) cultural, (7) interpersonal, and (8) adaptive. Handling the manifold human responses from this point of view has proved to be extremely fruitful. However, this is to be understood as a method of analysis, not a series of models.

The view of what man might become derives from psychotherapeutic practice, and leads toward an image of an "analytic ideal." This states that man can find the greatest degree of happiness if he loves, has pleasure, allows himself sexual gratification, has a wide range of feelings yet is guided by reason, has a role in a family, plays a part in a larger social structure, has a sense of identity, can communicate with his fellow men, is creative, and is free from psychiatric symptomatology. It is this image of the human estate that has been the most powerful lodestar attracting people from all cultures to Freud and psychoanalysis.

Another way of looking at it is this: man seeks happiness, yet for the most part he finds unhappiness. Conflict results, though there are varying areas of functioning which are conflict-free. The determination of what is conflicted and what is conflict-free is an empirical problem that cannot be solved by any general theory. The fact that one of man's devices for handling conflict is to conceal it from either himself or his fellow men or both increases enormously the problems associated with research and empirical observation. But it should not be held to alter the theory.

The role of the conceptual framework in the structure of science has tended to be ignored by many theoreticians, particularly those who write about scientific method in psychology. Hanson (1965) has shown how vital it is in all the physical sciences. Psychoanalytic conceptions have proved to be so useful that large numbers have already passed over into the popular vocabulary.

PSYCHOLOGY AND PHILOSOPHY

The hoary joke has it that in the nineteenth century psychology lost its soul, in the twentieth its mind. Gradually it is regaining its mind, and soon it will have a soul again. The divorce of philosophy from psychology was perhaps a necessary step in the development of an empirical science (Murphy, 1972). But it has gone much too far. Pure empiricism without any philosophical presuppositions is but another of those comforting illusions that scientists who like to perch in ivory towers employ to rationalize their preferences.

Values must be stated, even if they cannot be demonstrated to be best beyond the shadow of a doubt. The statement of the analytic ideal presents the values inherent in psychoanalysis.

The structure of psychological theory as it evolves from these considerations is as follows. Each component of the analytic ideal has to be understood both from a psychological and a philosophical point of view. What man does or has done must be compared with what he might do. No bit of behavior or experience can be considered apart from the setting in which it occurs, even the simplest. Since the human being is always striving for happiness, which in practice means that he is always struggling with certain conflicts, the relevance of any action to these conflicts must always be borne in mind.

Out of these analyses more general theories or laws could crystallize. Such a result is desirable but not absolutely necessary. It would appear that psychology is preeminently a field where generalizations are decidedly hazardous. That does not disqualify the science, it merely characterizes the field.

After a hundred years of intensive work by thousands of gifted investigators, the number of available laws in psychology is pitifully small; one may question whether there are any at all, except as guides to research. Such a result only points to the flexibility of the human being, indicating that physiological needs are more imperative than psychological, or rather that they permit fewer modes of gratification.

No theory can be expected to prove everything that it sets forth. The structure of psychology, as here presented, often rests on wide areas of reasonable inference. E.g., at an early date Freud recognized that a comparison of the productions of schizophrenics, dreamers, children, and primitives (later called "preliterates") could be extremely useful. Psychoanalytic investigators have followed his lead and have indeed come up with many useful discoveries. In most cases the attempt to translate these discoveries into hypotheses to be subjected to experimental test has proved to be an exercise in futility. Nor could it have been or be otherwise, since the variability is too complex to allow for real experimentation.

On the other hand, integration of material from many different sources has proved to be quite productive. This is the major methodological approach adopted in the present work. Gather data, wherever they are available, then integrate them into a coherent whole, guided by a conceptual framework that makes sense.

CHAPTER 2

The Meaning of Love in Human Experience

LOVE AS MAN'S CENTRAL EXPERIENCE

Love is the central experience of every individual's life in all cultures. Nevertheless, a satisfactory theory of love, one that gives adequate weight to all the physical, psychological, anthropological, and social factors involved, has not yet been formulated.

To begin with, four observations can be made. First, love makes people happy. As Freud once said, everybody knows this except the scientists. Hence the normal person is the one who can work and love. Second, the peculiarities of the love life can be traced back to the vagaries of childhood. Third, although love ideally makes people happy, the expressions of love which are encountered in the clinical situation are neurotic in nature, that is, immature. While psychoanalysts have spent much time discussing the immature, they have said relatively little about the mature forms of love. Hence the enormous gaps and disagreements in the theories. And fourth, in the course of psychoanalysis there is a progression from immature to mature love. If this progression succeeds, as it does in the majojrity of cases, then the individual knows more happiness than he has ever known before.

In the meantime many data relevant to the problem of love have been accumulated from many other sources. Anthropology, ethnology, child psychology, history have all uncovered facts of considerable importance. Clinical experience has also grown enormously. The findings from all these sources must be integrated.

Let us begin with the clinical experiences of the psychoanalyst. Freud and others have described a variety of clinical manifestations of love which are neurotic in character. After a brief initial euphoria, they result in a considerable amount of unhappiness. The study of these experiences makes up a considerable portion of the analytic work.

(a) *Love as a rescue fantasy.* This notion comes from the first of Freud's three essays in *Contributions to the Psychology of Love* (1910). Usually it is found among men, but it is also seen in women. The man wishes to rescue the woman from her unhappy lot. Hence he is apt to pick women who are realistically unhappy, or social deviants, such as prostitutes. These women are mother substitutes; in the family the mother is seen as an unhappy woman, who is made miserable by the brutal father. Sex is forced on her by the man, who uses her as a "spittoon."

In reality the woman who comes into marriage unhappy sooner or later brings this unhappiness back to the surface. The man begins to regret the sacrifices, often considerable, that he has made to rescue the woman. A rift results, which increasingly widens with time, especially after children come.

Of obvious significance in this kind of love, as in all the other neurotic forms described here, is the debased position assigned to sexuality. Love is "clean"; sex is "dirty." In this way the various forms of neurotic love all derive from an unresolved incestuous fixation in the Oedipal situation.

(b) *Love based on sexual debasement of the object.* In the culture of the antisexual family (the hate culture—this concept will be elaborated more fully later), the boy cannot believe that his mother would willingly engage in any such filthy activity as sex. Hence he splits off the object into the good and the bad: the good woman, who is the virginal mother, forced into sex by the sadistic father, and the bad woman, the "tramp," who is completely different from the mother. One is for love, the other is for sex, and never the twain shall meet. In this kind of atmosphere, the prophecy becomes self-fulfilling: the twain never do meet.

Here love is based on sexual denial very directly. Unconsciously the woman, who as a student of practicing psychology knows that she must play the role in order to get her man, comes to adopt the role more and more. She finds that if she is sexually responsive the man objects; she is a "bad" woman. So she remains cold and frigid. "Love" is maintained, but at the cost of sexual frustration for all. Incidentally, in these cases the man is likewise sexually inadequate and hides his inadequacy behind his emphasis on the virtuous woman.

(c) *Love for the virgin.* This category is related to the previous one. It is permissible to love a virgin, but not any other woman. In some cases it is even forbidden to love a woman who has previously been married.

The psychology of this situation from the woman's point of view was described by Freud in his paper "The Taboo of Virginity" (1918). He took up the primitive practice of defloration of the virgin (bride in some cases) by a senior man of the tribe, and ascribed it to the hostility of the woman toward the first man who possesses her. He says nothing, however, about the hostility of the man. Both of these attitudes are part of the anti-sexual hate culture.

(d) *Love as a defense against homosexuality.* This is one form of Don Juanism or its counterpart, nymphomania. Excessive sexual activity without real pleasure is engaged in to prove that the man is not a homosexual. (If there is a great deal of sexual activity with much pleasure it should not be described as Don Juanism.) As Freud pointed out in the Schreber case (1911), the formula is "I (a man) love another man," and it can be negated in various ways. One of them is to say: "I love a woman." Clinically in a number of these patients the homosexuality sooner or later becomes manifest.

(e) *Homosexual love.* Homosexual love involves first of all a denial of the opposite sex. When the partnership is examined more closely, a considerable amount of hatred becomes manifest. These liaisons are notoriously brief and unstable. Further, the two are usually acting out a mother-child relationship.

(f) *Love as dependency.* This is found more often among women than among men, though it is seen in both sexes. Love takes the form of submission. I will do anything for you; just love me in return. In these relationships, the increasing dependency of the lover becomes more and more intolerable.

This kind of dependency is the one that is historically most closely identified with love, and thus culturally the most common type. In its more masochistic form, to which it almost invariably turns, it becomes the search for the unattainable.

Andreas Cappellanus, in *The Art of Courtly Love* (1180), defines love as masochistic dependency in these words (p. 2):

Love is a certain inborn suffering derived from the sight of and excessive meditation upon the beauty of the opposite sex, which causes each one to wish above all things the embraces of the other and by common desire to carry out all of love's precepts in the other's embrace.

Masochistic dependency in love is linked with depression. Clinically, love and depression often go hand in hand.

(g) *Love as a transference.* The numerous varieties of love seen in people can be summed up under the concept of transference. The above are simply special cases. There is an almost innumerable variety of these transferences, all of which can be understood in the light of the idiosyncrasies of each person's childhood background.

So much for the varieties of love. But there is another side to the clinical picture: the abandonment of neurotic love and the growth toward healthy love. The characteristics of healthy love, as we see it developing in analysis, are primarily its greater hold on reality. Healthy love leads to pleasure and happiness; neurotic love leads to pain and unhappiness. The shift to mature love thus involves the consistent analysis of the painful elements in the present love.

In this connection, perhaps the two most common types of problems encountered in clinical practice can be mentioned. One is the *schizoid* man, who is unable to love a woman. The other is the *masochistic woman*, who confuses love with suffering and dependency. In both, love is a search for the unattainable. The more unattainable the love object, the more lovable he or she seems. Conversely, as soon as the love object is secured, it loses its fascination, and a deep disillusionment sets in.

HISTORICAL DATA

There is by now much information available about the historical development of the modern concepts of love, especially in Western society. The best summary is to be found in a work by Morton Hunt, *The Natural History of Love* (1959). I shall follow Hunt's outline here, with some emendations.

Hunt describes eight periods in Western history, from the Greeks to the present day. Each has struggled with the problem, and come up with a different solution. But all can be understood in terms of Freud's formulations of the development of sexuality toward mature love, or the union of tender and sexual feelings toward a person of the opposite sex.

(a) *The Greeks.* The Greeks had two names for love: *eros,* or carnal love, and *agape,* or spiritual love. In both of these a lowly state was ascribed to women and marriage.

(b) *The Romans.* The Romans took over the contempt for women that was characteristic of the Greeks, though not the homosexuality until much later. Sex was for man's pleasure; women should submit. But to this they added the Roman specialty of cruelty.

(c) *Early Christian asceticism.* In reaction against the sadism and sexual profligacy of the Romans, the Christians at first tried to abolish all sex. There was the institution of the continent marriage, then the spiritual marriage. In both cases there was either little or no sex. They even set up the "trial of chastity," which required two people to sleep together and yet remain chaste.

(d) *The creation of the romantic ideal.* Historians have been able to trace the origin of the romantic ideal to the end of the eleventh century. In southern France the game of courtly love became a reality. The treatise by Andreas Capellanus, cited earlier, became one of its major texts. Since then men and women throughout the Western world still live by and take for granted a number of its principal concepts.

One of the major tenets of courtly love was that it could not exist between man and wife. Love and sex were thus sharply differentiated. It is here that the image of the unattainable woman, the beautiful virgin, arises. Perhaps it is some corporealization of the Virgin Mary.

The romantics even continued the old game of temptation, making a game of what they called *amor purus,* in which the lover and his lady played around in bed in the nude without consummating the act. This was considered the highest achievement.

(e) *The lady and the witch.* Perhaps in inevitable reaction to this idealization of the woman came a period in which there was another sharp cleavage, but this time with intense persecution of the "bad" woman, the "witch." In the *Malleus maleficarum* (Kramer and Sprenger, 1486), the inquisitors' handbook of witchcraft persecution (which was also a textbook of psychiatry for several centuries), a whole delusional pattern of persecuting women was codified. It was a handbook religiously adhered to for several centuries; it had its heyday from 1500 to 1700.

(f) *Puritanism.* Although Puritanism is usually regarded as an antisexual reaction, this picture turns out to be historically incorrect. It was more an attempt to create a married love that would make both people happy, and a married love that was quite compatible with sexual pleasure.

(g) *The contact of two epidermises* (the eighteenth century). "Love," said Jonathan Swift in 1723, "is a ridiculous passion which hath no being but in play-books and romances." (Incidentally, his father died before he was born, his mother separated from him while he was still an infant, he never know the love of a mature woman, and he became psychotic in his old age.)

(h) *The angel in the house* (nineteenth century). This is the title of a book by Coventry Patmore, the spokesman for Victorian England. Victorianism represented an attempt to restore married life; it sought to combine love and sexuality in marriage. To do so the sexual excesses of the past had to be strictly banned. To the Victorian mind the free enjoyment of sexuality was the surest path to the destruction of the home.

(i) *Contemporary times.* Hunt calls our age "by love obsessed." No more so than other ages, apparently. What is happening today —and it has been going on since Freud wrote—is an attempt to put the Freudian ideal into actuality, coupled with all the other problems that have beset modern man. Thus the problem still remains, as it always has historically, of how sex and love can best be combined in marriage, or some other satisfactory institution.

ANTHROPOLOGICAL DATA

The literature contains no consistent discussion of the anthropological investigations into love. Where they have occurred, they have centered on sex more than any other element of the love experience. What we are looking for must be put together from many sources.

LOVE CULTURES VS. HATE CULTURES

First, I should like to propose a fundamental distinction among cultures: love cultures and hate cultures. In the love cultures the greater emphasis is on feelings of tenderness, affection, gratification, cooperation, and all the other outgrowths of these sentiments. In the hate cultures the greater emphasis is on feelings of hatred, warfare, competition, achievement, success, and the like. Naturally, these descriptions are not absolute; probably no culture ever known has been completely characterized by either love or hate. But the balance of forces can be estimated as weighing more heavily on one side or the other. Thus our own culture must be considered a hate culture, though with many forces on the side of love.

A basic thesis is that all of experience must be evaluated differently in a love culture than in a hate culture. In the love culture, love is more diffuse, less intense, more gratifying, less ringed with violence (in cases of unfaithfulness or desertion, for example), and less confined to marriage. In the hate culture the opposite of all of these is true.

No doubt in view of all that is known about hostility, it will immediately be doubted that there is such a thing as a love culture. Yet the anthropological literature is replete with descriptions of such cultures.

Margaret Mead (1937) has analyzed thirteen cultures; the cooperative would come closer to a love culture, the competitive to a hate culture. Her major conclusions are these (p. 511):

> Strong ego development can occur in individualistic, competitive or cooperative societies.
>
> Whether a group has a minimum or a plentiful subsistence level is not directly relevant to the question of how cooperative or competitive in emphasis a culture will be.
>
> The social function of success and the structural framework into which individual success is fitted are more determinative than the state of technology or the plentifulness of food.
>
> There is a correspondence between: a major emphasis upon competition, a social structure which depends upon the initiative of the individual, an evaluation of property for individual ends, a single scale of success, and a strong development of the ego.
>
> There is a high correspondence between: a major emphasis upon cooperation, a social structure which does not depend upon individual initiative or the exercise of power over persons, a faith in an ordered universe, weak emphasis upon rising in status, and a high degree of security for the individual.

LOVE CULTURES

There are cultures in which the concept of warfare is so foreign to the people's thinking that they cannot even understand it when it is described to them. Ruth Benedict (in *Patterns of Culture*, 1934, p. 28) quotes Rasmussen, who told of the blankness with which the Eskimos met his exposition of our custom. Benedict herself says that she tried to talk of warfare to the Mission Indians of California, but it was impossible.

Margaret Mead struck new ground in *Coming of Age in Samoa* (1928) when she described the sexual freedom of the Samoans and their relative freedom from guilt and conflict. In the old Samoa there were, however, many expressions of hatred. It is interesting that the Samoans have been able, according to Mead, to absorb the positive values of Western civilization, and to ignore the negative ones.

Bengt Danielsson, in his study of the Polynesians (1956), summarizes as follows the main positive aspects of the Polynesian way of life: (1) consistent moral code, (2) positive attitude toward sexuality, (3) sexual instruction, (4) premarital intercourse, (5) realistic conception of love, (6) wide extramarital liberty, (7) polygamy, (8) easy childbirth.

Spiro (1957) has investigated the people of the island of Ifaluk in the Pacific. This group, though small (250-260 people), is especially interesting because of the apparent absence of aggression in their world (as with the Zuñis). The only expression of aggression that Spiro found was the fact that they believe in, and exorcise, malevolent ghosts. Otherwise the outstanding sentiment in their ethos is the feeling of kindliness. Obedience, to his surprise, was exacted by love rather than by reward or punishment. Spiro concludes that there is no such thing as the complete suppression of aggression, but misses the point of his own findings. It is possible to have a society with a minimum of hate, even though it is not entirely absent. Thus it is possible to set up categories of hate and love cultures, and the Ifaluk would certainly qualify as a love culture.

The sociologist William Goode (1959) has done considerable research in the subject of love. He summarizes his main conclusions as follows: (1) Falling in love is a universal psychodynamic potential in the human being. Most human beings in all societies are capable of it. It is not, as Ralph Linton asserted, a psychological abnormality about as common as epilepsy. (2) We must look for the ways in which this potential is handled to prevent a disruption of the family structure. (3) Far from being uncommon, love relationships are a basis of the final choice of mate among a large minority of the societies of the earth.

Marriage will be discussed in more detail later. But it is relevant now to put in proper historical perspective our present institution of monogamy. According to Malinowski (1963, p. 950):

> Monogamy as the unique and exclusive form of marriage, in the sense that bigamy is regarded as a grave criminal offense and a sin as well as a sacrilege, is very rare indeed. Such an exclusive ideal and such a rigid legal view of marriage is perhaps not to be found outside the modern, relatively recent development of West-

ern culture. It is not implied in Christian doctrine even. Apart from such isolated phenomena as the recent Church of Latter Day Saints (Mormons) and the heretical sect of Anabaptists (16th century), polygamy was legally practiced and accepted by the Church in the Middle Ages, and it occurs sporadically as a legal institution accepted by Church and State as recently as the middle of the 17th century. . . .

Monogamy as pattern and prototype of human marriage, on the other hand, is universal. The whole institution, in its sexual, parental, economic, legal and religious aspects, is founded on the fact that the real function of marriage—sexual union, production and care of children, and the cooperation which it implies—requires essentially two people, and two people only, and that in the overwhelming majority of cases two people only are united in order to fulfill these facts.

In summary, then:

1. We can distinguish love cultures and hate cultures.

2. In the love culture, feelings associated with love, such as affection, friendliness, tenderness, sexuality (in its tender aspects), cooperation, and the like are encouraged, and institutions in which these feelings can be expressed are built up.

3. In the hate culture, feelings of hatred, resentment, jealousy, revenge, competition, overachievement, and the like are encouraged and institutions in which these feelings can be expressed are built up.

4. While both love and hate feelings exist in every culture known, the balance of forces varies considerably from culture to culture. It is possible to make meaningful distinctions on this basis.

5. Psychological monogamy is a relatively recent development in human history. Its relationship to the love or hate balance of the culture must be fully explored.

ETHOLOGICAL DATA

Animal investigations have by now established the fact that affectional needs exist in a wide variety of mammals. Schaller (1965, p. 137) states that gorilla groups remain stable, on the whole, even though there may be no receptive females for months at a time, indicating that sex is of little or no importance here. "Gorillas always gave me the impression that they stay together because they like and know one another. The magnanimity with which Big Daddy shared his females with other males, even though some were only temporary visitors, helped to promote peace in the group." The law of the jungle is apparently cooperation as much as the survival of the fittest.

Best known is Harry Harlow's (1974) series of investigations on monkeys. He has shown the importance of the affectional system in rhesus monkeys, and its relationship to the early contact with the mother. Most significant is his finding that if infant monkeys are brought up with surrogate mothers, they do not reach normal heterosexual adjustment. Thus touch by the mother, fondling, care, as well as biochemical feeding, are of crucial significance.

Even in lower species, the significance of bodily contact is great. Rheingold (1963, p. 254) states: "No anthropomorphic intent to instruct need be invoked to demonstrate how maternal behavior can permit, increase, or prevent, for example, the infant's social experience with other members of the species, including his peers."

CHILD PSYCHOLOGY

Direct observation of children in the first year of life has yielded information of considerable importance. Spitz has summarized his well-known investigations in *The First Year of Life* (1965). In general, it seems well established that adequate maternal stimulation is an absolute necessity for the infant, diminishing in importance gradually as time goes on. This love for the mother is the basis for all later love relationships. Love for the mother is the result of the amount of love, both psychological and physical, which the mother gives the infant. Briefly stated, love grows out of adequate mothering, including physical contact. The significance of touch in the love relationship remains in fact great all through life, though never as great as in infancy.

PSYCHOANALYTIC VIEWS

The psychoanalytic theory of love has been obscured by the fact that most writers, from Freud on, have devoted a great deal of attention to the pathological manifestations of love, and very little to the healthy ones.

Freud himself merely stated that the normal person is the one who can work and love. He did define maturity as the union of tender and sexual feelings toward a person of the opposite sex (genitality). However, he stopped there and never elaborated the question further.

Fenichel and Sullivan both state that one can speak of love only when consideration of the object goes so far that one's own satisfaction is impossible without satisfying the object too (or Sullivan, 1940, pp. 42-43! When the satisfaction or the security of another person becomes as significant to one as one's own satisfaction or security, then the state of love exists). Fenichel goes on further to state that in love there must be either a kind of partial and temporary identification for empathic purposes which either exists alongside the object relationship or alternates with it at short intervals. We know nothing about the specific nature of this identification. We can only say that the experience of a full and highly integrated satisfaction facilitates it, and that genital primacy (ability to have an adequate orgasm) is the prerequisite for it. For the rest, Fenichel discusses only neurotic love.

The major criticism of this definition of love as the state where the other person becomes as important as oneself is that it is psychologically impossible for any extended period of time. It emphasizes particularly the devotional or parental aspect of love (see below), omitting the genetic and social determinants of love.

Balint (1953, pp. 100-101) has described a form of object love which is not linked to any of the erotogenic zones, but is something on its own. It is rooted in the instinctual interdependence of mother and child. He feels that this tie is severed by our civilization much too early.

Fromm (1956) has written more about mature love than other analytic authors. He views love as an active power in man, a power that breaks through the walls that separate man from his fellow men, which unites him with others. Love makes him overcome the sense of isolation and separateness, yet it permits him to be himself. Love is primarily giving. Common to all forms of love, besides giving, are care, responsibility, respect, and knowledge.

A serious defect in Fromm's theory is his overemphasis on giving. This is true of maternal love, but not of other forms of love, in which taking is just as important. In fact, one could say that Fromm misidentifies love with maternal love. Also, Fromm's account is primarily dynamic, leaving out of account all the other essential points of view of metapsychology: topographic, economic, structural, and so on.

In an important work, O. Pfister (1944) attempted a synthesis of the Christian and the analytic views of love. In a historical survey, he showed that whenever Christian love reached a dominating position, it never succeeded in maintaining its early vigor. It was beset by two dangers: that of a kind of fever associated with the formation of neuroses and the replacement of love by compulsive formations like dogmas, magic rites, and institutions; and on the other hand that of a kind of chill. Love was in danger of either burning or freezing to death. Pfister saw the solution as an emphasis on the basic ethical ideal in

Christianity, together with personal analysis: the triumph of Christianity could come, he felt, only if all Christians were psychoanalyzed.

AN INTEGRATIVE THEORY OF LOVE

An integrative theory of normal love must give due weight to all the clinical, historical, anthropological, ethological, and child-psychological observations that have been described. Like any other analytic theory, it must consider the topographic, economic, dynamic, genetic, structural, interpersonal, cultural, and adaptive aspects of the phenomenon.

Mature love reaches a conscious stage when the individual has control over his feelings. He is not carried away by love; he loves. In agreement with Fromm, we can say that love is an active force. Thus loving is healthy; "falling in love" is neurotic.

Genetically, love may be said to go through five stages: attachment, admiration, mutual enjoyment, intimacy, and devotion.

1. *Attachment.* The earliest form of love is certainly simple attachment, which has a definite biological and physiological basis. It is found in the higher animals, especially the primates, in clear-cut form. The attachment is both psychological and physical; at this stage they cannot be distinguished. It is attachment to a mother (we can say in general the mothering figure, but in the vast majority of cases it is the mother).

2. *Admiration.* With the Oedipal phase the element of admiration enters in. On a good pregenital base the consequence of development at this stage is a loving evaluation of the parents: they are bigger, stronger, kinder, and so on; hence admiration. In a loving family (a love culture), the normal result of the Oedipal period is penis pride, rather than castration anxiety, vaginal pleasure rather than penis envy. This phase lasts all through the latency period, and in greater or lesser degree is incorporated into all love relationships later on in life.

3. *Sexual enjoyment.* The next stage is that of puberty, with an outburst of sexual enjoyment. This is biologically determined, though it rests on the satisfactory resolution of the earlier stages, especially the attachment to the mother (as animal studies show too). Optimal for the development of the individual is a period of free sexual experimentation in adolescence. The anthropological evidence is overwhelming that this makes for healthy growth.

4. *Intimacy.* The period of sexual enjoyment is followed by inti-

macy primarily with one person of the opposite sex. This intimacy is on a more spiritual level; it includes a mutual interchange of feelings, hopes, attitudes, memories, dreams, and everything else that makes life worthwhile. Here for the first time the person really feels that he is an adult.

5. *Devotion*. This is the final stage, in which the emphasis is on the children. Devotion (which many authors have confused with the whole of love) requires a greater concern for the welfare of the other person than for one's own; this is not true of the earlier stages. It is not necessary that devotion should exclude pleasure and intimacy; in fact, most parent-child relationships suffer from too much devotion on the part of the parent, or rather devotion that places the needs of the parent before those of the child. But certainly the child is the weaker and more needy individual, and there are many times in the growth of any child when nothing more is required of the parent than simple devotion.

These five ingredients enter into the adult feeling of love. They can be mixed up in varying measures; these mixtures determine the sincerity and adequacy of any love relationship.

CHAPTER 3

Pleasure and Pain

Although it is one of the oldest observations that man seeks pleasure and avoids pain, the exact nature of pleasure and pain have never been adequately elucidated.

PHILOSOPHICAL VIEWS

Throughout the ages philosophers and psychologists have speculated about the nature of pleasure without reaching any substantial agreement. Six different positions have been taken: (1) *Bentham*: pleasure is the highest good; (2) *Aristotle*: happiness is the highest good; (3) *Plato*: mastery of man's lower nature; (4) *Stoicism*: suppression of desire; (5) *Mysticism*: happiness is a state independent of the external world; (6) *Kant*: happiness is unattainable, do your duty.

All of these positions have been continued in one form or another on the contemporary scene. Closest to Freud is the utilitarian position of Bentham; actually Freud took it over most directly from the Englishman and his collaborator John Stuart Mill, who was one of the heroes of his youth. Aristotle is continued in the self-actualization of Maslow. Plato and the Stoics are represented by philosophical positions that resign themselves to the evils of the world, and seek happiness elsewhere. Kant's emphasis on duty is echoed in many ways, including both democracy and totalitarianism.

What all these philosophers lack is an adequate psychological basis. Desire, pleasure, happiness cannot really be understood without reference to the unconscious, and the total ego structure, as well as the total social structure. Without adequate psychological understanding these positions become rationalizations of neurotic needs; with psychological understanding, as in hedonism or eudaemonism, they acquire a much deeper meaning in which the abstract philosophical discussion is subordinated to its role in the life of the individual. It is in this sense that psychoanalysis becomes a continuation of and an enrichment of philosophy (McGill, 1967).

FREUD AND POST-FREUDIAN VIEWS

The concept of a pleasure principle was basic to Freud's thinking from the very beginning. Yet, though he came to recognize the difficulties more and more as time went on, he never fully clarified all the problems inherent in it.

Much of the time Freud took a simple common-sense approach. In *Jokes and the Unconscious* (1905, p. 126) he wrote, "For man is a tireless pleasure-seeker—I forget where I came across this happy expression—and any renunciation of a pleasure he has once enjoyed comes hard to him."

Yet in his more systematic writings he proceeded along economic and metapsychological lines that contradicted or muddied the simple common-sense position. Originally he stressed the avoidance of unpleasure rather than the pursuit of pleasure, tying up these concepts with quantitative factors (Project, 1895). Eventually in his 1911 paper on the two psychic principles he used the term "pleasure principle" for the first time. Here he described a sequence in development from the pleasure to the reality principle (the two principles).

All this was tenable, and could have been worked out, had he not introduced the bombshell of the death instinct in *Beyond the Pleasure Principle* in 1920. Even though Freud, at first hesitant, grew more firmly convinced of the truth of his far-reaching speculations, others could not follow him. The concept of a death instinct, with the strange statement that "the aim of all life is death," is so contrary to all normal psychological and biological knowledge that one can only speculate on how a Freud could arrive at such a position. As Jones pointed out in 1957, by that time, of the fifty or so papers devoted to the topic in the first decade, half supported Freud's theory, in the second decade only a third, and in the last decade none at all.

From the collapse of the death instinct theory psychoanalysts could still rescue a basic instinctual drive of aggression. But whatever can be said about aggression, too little note has been taken of the fact that as far as Freud's total systematic structure is concerned, a clarification of the road from the pleasure principle to the reality principle, which later became from id to ego, has never been offered in a satisfactory way. Nor did Freud ever clear up any of the numerous thorny problems connected with this question. How is one pleasure to be distinguished from another? What is the metapsychology of pleasure? What is the relationship of pleasure to reality? What is the relationship of pleasure to consciousness? All these questions and many more must still be answered in a systematic theory of psychology.

Freud's followers could not go along with him in his biological speculations. Some merely ignored the question entirely. Others, like Fenichel (1945) and Schur (1966), essentially tried to get back to the earlier Freud. Since this leaves too many questions unanswered, it is likewise unsatisfactory.

TOWARD AN INTEGRATIVE THEORY

Although nothing is as simple as it appears, the simplest form of pleasure is still the basic physiological one. Unlike pain, however, pleasure is not associated with specific nerve pathways or parts of the body, but is a much more diffuse sensation. It appears that certain bodily areas are endowed with a multiplicity of nerve endings that make their stimulation highly pleasurable. This is true of the oral, anal, and phallic areas. To a lesser extent it is true of the other areas of the body, while it is also true that the exercise of almost any function can provide some pleasure. Further, many people have unusual sensitivities in certain parts of their bodies which are then known as erotogenic zones.

Still at the physiological level, four observations are pertinent. First, there are wide areas of physiological functioning which are entirely outside the ability of the body to report to the brain. These processes, such as digestion or circulation, become noticeable only when they are disturbed, and even then only in indirect ways ("referred" pain). In general the satisfactory maintenance of these nonreported physiological processes leads to a broad sense of well-being, while their frustration leads to a sense of dis-ease. At the same time these feelings of well-being and dis-ease occur only in the course of time, and are not directly related by the individual to immediate pleasure or pain. Thus in a goodly number of cases severe illness or death may result without any previous warning signs. Thus pleasure is only in a broad sense an indication of well-being; it is rather well-being that leads to a heightened sense of pleasure. Pleasure then becomes a "peak experience" that may or may not lead to optimal well-being for the individual.

It is here that the reality principle enters in the form of anticipations of the future, based on better knowledge. Many forms of immediate gratification prove harmful in the long run; the individual must adjust himself accordingly. Indeed, all the major forms of pleasure require a certain amount of constraint for their fullest enjoyment; the rational restraints intermingle with social and intrapersonal desires and constraints to form an essential part of the personality. In one sense this point had already been anticipated by the philosophical discussions.

Second, many of these areas of well-being are not immediately obvious to the ordinary individual, but must be taught by older persons or as a result of scientific research. Acquired tastes become as significant a source of desire as unlearned ones. Thus pleasure and well-being become much more complex entities than the philosophers had thought. As time went on, Freud recognized this as well, but he never confronted the problem in any satisfactory way.

Third, since the 1940s it has been realized that understimulation can be as bad for the individual as overstimulation (Zubek, 1969). This late discovery has never been adequately integrated into psychological theory.

Fourth, the need-reduction model of pleasure, common to both classical psychoanalysis and behaviorism, is an oversimplification. Even at the simple physiological level it is misleading.

The basic physiological model should be seen as a cycle of need-gratification-rest-need, rather than a hypothetical state of constant equilibrium. The image of homeostasis, which describes the constant inner state of the organism, thus has to be modified. Freud accepted it through his carry-over of Fechner's law of constancy, hence his emphasis on the avoidance of unpleasure rather than the pursuit of pleasure. In the homeostatic view a need serves as a disrupter, a disturber of the peace, which has to be "reduced" and expelled as soon as possible. Hence to live without needs seems like the *summum bonum*. In fact the concept does derive historically from the religious image of calm and contentment, in which the ideal man is something like a Buddha perennially looking at his navel, and happy with

what he sees. Such a position ignores the harmful effects of understimulation.

By contrast, in the cyclical image of pleasure, needs are just as
important as a state of rest. Relaxation without any intrusion by
needs has always been upheld as a "saintly" way to live in many
cultures and by many religious groups. It is notorious that the vast
mass of men are unable to comply with such an ideal, the simplest
explanation for which is that it is too foreign to human nature. Living
organisms have needs; they can be manipulated, transformed, subli-
mated, repressed, and handled in many other ways, but sooner or later
they make themselves manifest.

It is of interest that a coalescence of views appears to be taking
place on this score. The change in psychoanalytic thinking has been
noted above. In the behavioristic camp need-reduction has likewise
come to be seen as an oversimplified position (Cofer and Apley,
1964). Kimble (1973) outlined three interpretations of the critical
factor in reinforcement: (1) tension reduction; (2) consummatory
behavior, whose occurrence could conceivably have reinforcement
value greater than that of other stimuli involving equal amounts of
consummatory behavior; and (3) reinforcing stimuli.

EMPIRICAL DATA ON PLEASURE AND ITS GRATIFICATION

1. *The pleasure-seeker.* Perhaps most significant is the impressive
body of clinical and empirical data showing that the persistent pleasure-seeker (self-styled) is often a most disturbed individual, who ends
up in serious trouble. Though originally he was designated an "im-
pulsive" (*Triebhafte*) character, in more recent years everything has
been dumped into the rubric of the "acting-out" personality. Typically, the acting-out personality (1) is orally fixated, (2) has a low
frustration tolerance, (3) is highly anxious, and (4) has a weak ego.

2. *The social-historical-familial suppression of pleasure.* Historically
and currently society, chiefly through the family as intermediary,
exerts a strong influence to suppress many pleasurable activities. The
degree of such suppression has varied all over the lot during the
course of human history, ranging from extreme permissiveness to
tyrannical prohibition. From a theoretical point of view two comments are significant: first of all it is possible to suppress a considerable part of the pleasurable activities of men (though not without
harmful effects); and second, the greater the suppression, the greater
the force, both physical and ideological, needed to maintain it.

3. *Mental illness as the fear of pleasure.* Much clinical evidence has accumulated indicating that a powerful fear of pleasure leads to varying degrees of mental illness. Rado (1956) postulated a *congenital anhedonia* in the schizophrenic. The congenital or genetic basis is dubious, but the observation is correct. Jones (1948) suggested the term "aphanisis" to describe the complete deprivation of all pleasure which is so feared by the child. Generally speaking, it is the harsh superego that lies at the base of all severe mental disturbance (Fenichel, 1945; Nunberg, 1955).

On the basis of these and related empirical data, the variations from the basic model and its later development can be conceptualized as follows:

IMBALANCE

Problems arise when there is some imbalance in the cyclical pattern of need and satisfaction. This imbalance can, to begin with, take one of four forms:

1. *Disturbances in need.* The person can experience too much need or too little need. Traditionally it is only the individual who experienced too much need who was seen as "sick" or in need of explanation; this was a social bias that blocked knowledge. Of the two modes of relating to the mother, the symbiotic and the autistic, the symbiotic expresses too much need, the autistic too little, but both deviations have dire consequences.

2. *Disturbances in gratification.* Some individuals have intense "peak experiences"; others feel very little gratification from the satisfaction of their desires. Sometimes gratification may be entirely absent; these are the "anesthetic" individuals. Localized anesthesias may also occur in many people; this was one of the first symptoms that drew the attention of physicians in Freud's day. Optimally gratification must range between certain limits; too much or too little both imply the complication of the pleasure by internalized psychic factors.

3. *Disturbances in rest.* A period of quiescence is part of the physiological pattern. Most often it is a period of sleep, as in infancy, following the feeding experience. Later on there are the symptoms of hypersomnia (too much sleep), as contrasted with too little (insomnia). Sleep disturbances at all ages are extraordinarily widespread.

4. *Disturbances in recurrence of the cycle.* Biological clocks appear to govern many of the basic physiological activities, in spite of all

individual differences. Too much variation does not seem to be within the expected range of human experience. Hence after rest the need will reassert itself after a reasonable amount of time. If it recurs too quickly, the rest is disturbed; if too slowly, the rest is too prolonged.

NEED REDUCTION

Need reduction remains one form of pleasure, but not the whole of it. Two forms can be distinguished: the positive, in which some normal physiological need occurs and is gratified, as in hunger, and the negative, where there is avoidance of a noxious stimulus, as in pain.

PLEASURE GAIN

Once the basic needs are satisfied, the human being is faced with a wide variety of choices. One is to increase the range of his pleasures. Such an increase would rest on pleasure gain rather than need reduction. In his book *The Importance of Living* (1937), Lin Yutang has provided an eloquent description of the many ways in which life happiness can be expanded along these lines.

ACTING-OUT

Repressed desires can be handled by a variety of defense mechanisms, but for present purposes acting-out remains the most important. In acting-out the person handles some pressing desire by action rather than by reflection. Analytic scrutiny indicates that many of the pleasure-seekers are acting-out their desires, rather than experiencing true pleasure.

ALTERATIONS OF CONSCIOUSNESS VS. PLEASURE

Many apparent forms of pleasure, upon closer examination, turn out to lead to altered states of consciousness (ASCs). This is particularly true of the drugs that have had such a vogue in recent years. In other words, no pleasure can really be understood properly without reference to the total ego structure (Holt et al., 1972).

CONCLUDING REMARKS ON THE PLEASURE PRINCIPLE

Clinical and empirical experience with a variety of forms of pleasure reinforces the theoretical position adopted here. Even though food, drugs, sex, bodily activity, and other seemingly simple physical pleasures are touted over and over again as the answer to happiness, on closer examination it appears that all are indulged in by people for a variety of reasons. Excesses in particular, in whatever area, are apt to prove damaging.

Thus the pleasure principle, as a result of early experiences, becomes molded into a series of wishes, which have a complex structure. These wishes become the true determining forces for action as well as for ideation (fantasy), rather than the original pleasurable desire. Another way of putting this is to say that the id has its dynamics, and is rarely seen in pure form after early childhood. As a theoretical principle the search for pleasure remains valid. But for the practical motivations that lead to everyday activities it is necessary to look to the wishes and their deep intertwinings with the ego structure. Thus the road from the pleasure principle to the reality principle, which Freud pointed to but did not sketch in any detail, has to be sought in the development of the ego and of the entire personality structure.

PAIN

From a theoretical point of view the observations on pain run parallel to those on pleasure. Whatever claims are made one way or the other, it is the ego structure that is decisive for the perception and transformation of pain in the psyche.

Purely physiological pain may be so excruciating that it takes over the entire functioning of the individual. Yet clinical data on masochism show not only that some persons can tolerate inordinate amounts of pain but even that they seek it out in preference to pleasure. Hence pain can be regarded as a basic psychosomatic mechanism (Sternbach, 1968).

Originally "false" reports of pain, i.e., pain in the absence of demonstrable organic cause, were referred to as "hysterical." Even at an early date Freud had elucidated the essential mechanism of these pains (*Studies in Hysteria*, 1895): they are means of communicating distress because other means of communication have been blocked by the superego. They must be distinguished from true psychosomatic events in which there is actual damage to the tissues.

Once the psychogenic nature of these pains was understood, their relationship to the ego structure came under investigation. Here the concept of "somatization" was developed. There are people who express their feelings through bodily symptoms because other expressions come to be forbidden to them for historical reasons. Schur (1955) has suggested that in the normal individual the course of development runs from an early stage in which psychic and physiological perceptions are merged (similar to Piaget's sensorimotor stage), roughly the first two years of life, to one in which the psychological and the physiological can be increasingly differentiated. He calls this process *desomatization*. In the psychosomatic individual, the process is reversed, and a *resomatization* takes place.

CHAPTER 4

Instinct and Feeling

The question of what human nature is is fundamental to all psychology. Historically, psychoanalysis, stressing instinctual behavior, has been opposed by behaviorism, stressing the environmental influences. Both of these positions represent oversimplifications. By now evidence is available from many sources, and has to be solidified into a coherent theory.

LEARNING AND INISTINCT

Experimental work with animals justifies the following conclusions:

1. Instinctive behavior can be adequately defined and profitably studied in a variety of animal species.

2. All behavior is affected by both internal and external causes.

3. Instinctual behavior is species-specific.

4. Social behavior frequently overrides the inner needs of any animal organism, even at fairly low levels of evolution.

5. No generalizations about instincts for all species are warranted by the present state of scientific knowledge.

6. Extrapolation from animal behavior to human is speculative at best. The major difference lies in the much higher degree of mentalization of the human being.

Experimental psychology and learning theory have, as is well known, long been opposed to instinct theory and strongly environmentalist in their orientation. The general position, the extreme of which today is found perhaps in B. F. Skinner, is that all behavior is learned, and that all that the scientist has to do is to find the right schedules of reinforcement to get the animal to perform as he wishes. This applies to human as well as to infrahuman species.

Against this extreme position an increasing number of learning theorists are beginning to rebel. In a recent review of scientific psychology in transition, Gregory Kimble (1973, pp. 17-18) first points out that the traditional attempts to derive laws of learning of great generality have failed, and that the extreme environmentalist position is untenable. He concludes that psychology is in a position now to investigate problems that were once considered illegitimate on methodological grounds. These include important aspects of personal experience, unusual psychological states, and causes that until recently seemed beyond us.

In the meantime, further work in anthropology has led to several unexpected conclusions. First of all, all human societies have to cope with certain ineluctable demands, which are best described in terms of psychoanalytic instinct theory: sexuality, hostility, anxiety, and their correlates. Second, these demands can be met in a large variety of ways, and have been so met. Third, and perhaps most important, whatever organized system for approaching human needs is adopted by a given culture becomes an imperative command for the members of that culture.

The development of clinical psychoanalysis has also led to some noteworthy results. Sexuality, following Freud's developmental scheme, moves from narcissism to a stage of genital love, in which there is a union of tender and sexual feeling toward a person of the opposite sex. Anxiety, following Freud's second theory (which is virtually universally accepted today), is prototypically separation anxiety; the greatest fear is separation from the mother. Hostility is directed most strongly at other people.

Further, sexuality can be directly traced to the maturation of the various parts of the body, including release of various hormones in the course of development. By contrast, in spite of extensive research, no physiological state has been shown to exist which per se makes the person anxious or hostile. But the opposite is often true: hostility and anxiety have considerable somatic consequences, quite often very severe in nature.

No one today would venture to say with Freud that in studying human beings we are contributing to biology. Our knowledge is limited to humans, and our concern must be with setting up an instinct theory that applies to humans. Inasmuch as ethologists have demonstrated that instinct theory must be species-specific, this seems like a perfectly justifiable demand.

Accordingly, for human beings a definition can be offered as follows:

An instinct is an unlearned drive, with a conative-affective core, based on preformed neurophysiological structures, which links the somatic with the psychic, and the individual with the social.

In accordance with this definition, two types of instincts can be distinguished: constructive and reactive. The constructive instincts are those that tend to arise spontaneously in a favorable secure environment; essentially this is sexuality. The reactive instincts are those that are aroused in reaction to some frustrating stimulus, but once aroused they have enormous force. These would include hostility and anxiety. Accordingly we arrive at three major instincts in the human being: sexuality, hostility, and anxiety; or, in more popular language, love, hate, and fear.

INSTINCT AND FEELING

The Sandler-Joffe distinction between experience and theory must be brought into play here. In theory these are the three instincts that play major roles in human behavior. But in practice what is dealt with is the experience that the individual undergoes. Primarily this experience consists of a variety of affects. These affects do not "derive" from the instincts, as some theoreticians put it; that confuses experience and theory (cf. Melanie Klein's confused notion that the death instinct turned inward creates anxiety). The affects are primary; hence the various attempts to "define" them have led to nothing beyond intuitive understanding. Or put another way, these affective reactions are inevitable in human experience. They seem to conform to certain general laws that can be spelled out fairly clearly. And it is possible to build up a coherent theory of human experience based on the ways in which these affects are handled by the person and by the culture.

It is not generally realized that Freud, in drawing a sharp distinction between drive and affect, was merely echoing the prevailing theory of his day (Fletcher, 1957). Since his real contribution lay elsewhere, the elimination of this distinction serves to reconcile the theory with the information that has accumulated since then.

THE ID: A RECONSIDERATION

In the light of what is now known about the instincts, a reconsideration of Freud's concept of the id is in order. Freud packed too much into it. The id should be regarded as a locus where certain reactions take place. Furthermore, clear distinctions must be drawn, which Freud did not do, between past and present, as well as between drive and unconscious.

THE HUMAN INSTINCTS (BASIC FEELINGS)

Since instinct must be approached in a species-specific way, it is best to confine ourselves to those that are operative in the human being. It requires additional research to clarify how much the human being has or does not have in common with the lower animals.

In what follows instinct and feeling are used synonymously, in accordance with the discussion above. This allows for a clarification of the mainstream of human experience. It should be borne in mind that in the discussion of feeling, the underlying metapsychological approach, embracing the topographic, genetic, dynamic, structural, and other points of view (cf. Chapter 1), must be given full consideration.

THE NEED FOR DISCHARGE

Traditionally it has been held that the instincts have a peremptory character, forcing a discharge of some kind. McDougall adopted the rather simplistic view that these discharges affected behavior fairly directly. Freud introduced a number of subtleties into the observation. For him the discharge may be psychic or it may be somatic, it may be conscious or it may be unconscious, it may be fairly directly observable or it may be woven into the personality structure in such subtle and devious ways that only an intricate uncovering of all the associations can lead to the awareness of some instinctual impulse at the end of the chain. In general, the immediate discharge calls up the secondary process. The interplay between the primary and secondary processes, in which the immediate instinctual demands are held in check by ego apparatuses, accounts for a good deal of personality functioning.

The variations of discharge and control make up the ego structure. In this respect a considerable degree of plasticity is observable in the human being, the limits being set only by the existence of the fundamental instincts. However, this plasticity is further limited by the culture in which the individual is brought up. Certain combinations of discharge and control become incorporated in the individual's psyche from an early age as a result of the family structure, the representative of the culture in which he is reared. Once this personality pattern is formed, it is extremely difficult to get away from it, even when the person consciously wants to.

While the instinctual needs are in this way subordinated within the total ego structure, their control is never entirely adequate. The "return of the repressed" is a constant phenomenon. Thus, regardless of the ego structure, instinctual material tends to break through to consciousness, where it has to be handled anew with a variety of defense measures. This is one important factor that leads to the degree of tension or conflict the individual experiences.

The principle should actually be reformulated into continual discharge of instinctual needs. To speak of a "need" for discharge is too teleological. It is more correct to speak of the discharge principle per se. Some of this discharge comes from present-day physiological needs, some from past, and some from the complex transformations that the instinctual needs undergo psychically.

MENTALIZATION

Since the instinct represents one linkage between the somatic and the psychic, it readily lends itself to a process of mentalization. By this is meant that from a very early stage the instincts become intertwined inextricably with the mental apparatus. As the person grows older this mentalization becomes more and more prominent because of increasing control (ego strength) and because of the increasing capacity for mental activity. From a fairly early stage physiology releases the impulse but psychology determines what happens to it. This is why it is so difficult to see the id in pure form; it is rather an inference from a variety of observations.

A certain amount of mental life, varying with the individual and his ego structure, develops as a result of primary ego autonomy. The available evidence indicates that with a secure early environment, ego autonomy reaches a height; with an insecure one, it becomes more and more dependent on the instincts. Besides this autonomous mental functioning, there is the psychic reflection or reverberation of the instinctual life. How much of the mental life is taken up by instinctual representations, and how much by autonomous factors, is hard to say. In general, pre-Freudian authors tended to exaggerate the role of the autonomous ego; Freud and post-Freudian authors have tended to underestimate its significance. Much research has been done on this topic, which will be summarized in Chapter 8.

SOCIALIZATION

Since the instinct is a link between the individual and the social, it necessarily plays a vital role in the process of socialization which is at the heart of all cultures. The exact nature of the interaction between instinct and culture remains to be clarified, however.

A number of persistent questions are found throughout all discussions. How much variability is possible in the regulation of the instinctual drives? Here a clear-cut answer is possible: A great deal, but not limitless. Anthropological research has established that the variations are so wide that they have led to a theory of cultural relativity, in which everything is presumably subject to cultural influences. But this goes too far.

CAPACITY FOR FRUSTRATION

In spite of the peremptory character of instinctual drives, the human being's capacity to frustrate them is enormous. In fact, it is precisely because of this capacity for frustration, and the consequent variability among cultures, that the instincts play such an important role. By contrast, if certain vital foods are not provided, the individual and the culture simply die.

NATURE OF INSTINCTUAL GRATIFICATION

Under what circumstances can an instinctual need be said to be satisfied? Here the various instinctual needs have to be evaluated differently.

Sexuality readily lends itself to the paradigm for pleasure described in Chapter 3: need-gratification-rest-need. Persistent lack of gratification is a neurotic symptom rather than something inherent in sexuality per se.

However, this is not true for the other two instincts. Neither hostility nor anxiety can be made to conform to this model. Rather they obey a kind of unpleasure principle, where the person is impelled to get rid of the danger by fight (hostility) or flight (anxiety); nor is it any accident that these two are so close together that theoreticians today talk of the flight-fight syndrome. Further, the simple release of hostility or anxiety is not per se pleasurable, contrary to what many allege; what is true rather is that many people find it hard to control these feelings.

After a certain point both hostility and anxiety are directed primarily at internal rather than external objects. Once that happens, the person struggles heroically against these introjects, without ever being able to rid himself of them. From that point on the gratification of hostility or anxiety is a pseudogratification, since the introject, the real culprit, is never removed. In realistic situations what is needed is a removal of the stimulus that leads to the affective reaction. Over and beyond that, after a certain point only an inner psychological reconstruction is of any value.

ACTING-OUT

Because of the difficulties involved in achieving real gratification, a distinction must be drawn between real satisfaction and acting-out. Acting-out gives temporary relief without lasting satisfaction. Further, as a rule the acting-out is carried out without regard to the reality of the consequences, thus giving rise to many of the most disturbing personal and social problems.

Much, perhaps most, of what has been called instinctual gratification in the past is really a form of acting-out. A satisfactory differentiation can be made only on the basis of a full knowledge of the individual.

INTERCHANGEABILITY: DISPLACEMENT

One of the most significant aspects of the psychology of the instincts is their interchangeability or displaceability. Thus hostility may express sexuality, or vice versa. It is noteworthy that in English the word "fuck" is rarely used in any but a hostile connotation. Likewise anxiety and hostility, as well as anxiety and sexuality, may be interchanged with one another. Fusions of the various instincts are also found all the time. Thus here too the id is seen only in derivative form; what is id has to be inferred from all the sources available.

NATURE OF DRIVE STRENGTH

For any given situation, what is it that determines the strength of any particular drive for a given individual? The approach to this problem via animal experimentation leads to no conclusions applicable to human beings.

In humans three factors are responsible: unconscious push, instinctual force, and historical antecedents (or pressures). It is not possible to generalize easily about which is more powerful. Different situations lend themselves to different resolutions. The "tyranny of the drives" can be underrated, as it was before Freud, or overrated, as it has been by many Freudian authors. The lack of clarity in Freud's concept of the id (see above)—for example, failing to distinguish between unconscious, past drives (childhood) and present physiological pressures—has led to some of the confusion in this area.

PSYCHIC ENERGY

The notion that the instincts dominate the whole of mental life by providing some "energy" that is deployed in many directions was common to all the early instinct theories, and was taken over by Freud from them. Many theoreticians today reject this concept as unverified by either clinical experience or theoretical necessity.

Applegarth (1971), summarizing more recent work, also shows that the concept of psychic energy is not compatible with what is known today of psychology and neurophysiology, so that it should accordingly be discarded.

As can be seen from various passages in the present work, whatever validity propositions regarding psychic energy may have can more profitably be formulated in other terms (see, for example, discussions of the pleasure principle in Chapter 3 and of sexuality in Chapter 5).

CHAPTER 5

Sexuality

Few topics in human psychology have been as extensively studied as sexuality. Material is available from many sources—clinical, experimental, anthropological, physiological, biological. Even more than in other areas the task of the theoretician is to evaluate the adequacy of the material, and to coordinate it into a meaningful whole.

In the *Three Essays on Sexuality* (1905), Freud demonstrated beyond the shadow of a doubt that the adult sex life of man is strongly influenced by the entire course of his development.

Three broad stages in human growth can be distinguished: infantile sexuality, from birth to five; the latency period, from five to puberty; and puberty, when sexuality in the adult sense matures. Conceptually, the sexual instinct must be divided into an aim and an object. The aim is the release of the sexual energy or products; the object is the person who gratifies this release, or toward whom the release is directed. Since an object is basically a person, this aspect of sexual development could just as well be referred to as the development of interpersonal relationships. Actually, such a terminology would have avoided the many sterile acrimonious disputes that have marred the field.

While the stages of development are chronologically determined, so much overlap occurs that they cannot be thought of as completely independent of one another. Accordingly the term "phase" has come

37

into common use. Reference is then made to phase-specific drives and activities.

INFANTILE SEXUALITY (BIRTH TO FIVE YEARS)

The period of infantile sexuality is further subdivided into three broad phases: the oral (birth to one year), the anal (one to three years) and the phallic (three to five). In terms of aim it proceeds from feeding to intercourse; in terms of object, or interpersonal relationship, from an indiscriminate reliance on the breast or its equivalent to a strong desire for the parent of the opposite sex.

In the course of growth other aspects of the personality develop— hostility, anxiety, the ego, the superego, the self-image, identifications, and so on. It is only for the sake of clarity of presentation that the present discussion is limited to the sexual factor; everything else is important as well, but can be touched upon only as it relates to sexuality.

THE ORAL PHASE (BIRTH TO ONE YEAR)

In the oral phase, the prime need of the infant, apart from the basic physiological requirements, is for the warmth and love of the mother (or a mother substitute, if the biological mother is for some reason not available).

That the human infant necessarily goes through a prolonged period of dependency on the mother (or a substitute) scarcely requires much proof, yet it is a fact that until comparatively recently this requirement for healthy living tended to be disregarded by many theoreticians. Even Freud saw as much danger in "spoiling" infants as in gratifying them, until he finally evolved his second theory of anxiety.

Maternal Attachment

While the attachment to the mother is indisputable, the reasons for this attachment have been the subjects of considerable debate. Common sense would dictate that it is based on the care and attention that the mother gives to the infant, yet the attachment seems to go well beyond that, and indeed there are other phenomena, such as the development of separation anxiety sometime in the first year of life, rather than immediately after birth, which do not fit in with an exclusive emphasis on physical care. Bowlby (1969, pp. 222-23) ascribes prime importance to *imprinting* rather than to the consequences of feeding and physical care. He also proposes an evolutionary hypothesis to account for the phenomenon.

Whatever the origins of attachment behavior may be, its vicissitudes can be more clearly traced than ever before. In the monkey Harlow (1974) has described the existence of five affectional systems: mother-child, child-mother, peer group, heterosexual, and paternal. Further he has shown that there is a biologically determined sequence to these systems, one passing on to the other whenever the previous one is sufficiently satiated or gratified. Should an earlier one be frustrated, for either natural or artificial reasons, there will be first an attempt to compensate, and second a negative reaction (read in humans: ego defect) leading the animal to deviate from normal development. Once maturity is reached, the cycle is repeated.

In principle the same cycle applies to humans, with the caveat of course that the human experience is far more complex. But there is a biologically determined attachment of infant to mother, which then proceeds in reasonably well-defined stages to a series of attachments throughout life. Ideally human life can be a series of loving experiences; obviously in practice it is not. The deviation of the practical human experience of many hatreds from the ideal of many loves is similar to the framework of this book, in which actual human experience is contrasted with the analytic ideal.

In the young infant (less than three months of age), attachment needs are so powerful that if they are thwarted, death (marasmus: Spitz) or very severe disturbance will follow, with rare exceptions. Schizophrenia, which should be regarded as *the* functional psychosis, may involve a regression to this stage (Melanie Klein, Sullivan, Burnham, Rheingold). The major etiological factor is the "bad breast" or the schizophrenogenic mother. Because of the immaturity of the psychic apparatus the concepts of primary narcissism (Freud) or infantile autism (Mahler) are misleading at this stage.

Some ego is present from birth (Stone et al., 1973). Its gradual growth and independence of the id can be described (Hartmann, Piaget). In the first year of life the ego is still rudimentary, accounting for the extreme vulnerability of the infant to all kinds of traumata, especially separation.

The infant suffers from terrible anxieties (Melanie Klein), which gradually diminish with the growth of the ego. Some developmental abnormalities occur in almost everybody (Brody and Axelrod, 1970), though the more secure the environment, the fewer the abnormalities. At this stage it is impossible to distinguish between anxiety and hos-

tility, though anxiety seems more in evidence. Hence anxiety should
be regarded as instinctual. A maturational sequence of love-fear-hate
in monkeys has been described by Harlow.

The effects of any kind of stress (Selye, 1956) run parallel to
bad mothering, forming the basis for subsequent psychosomatic illnesses (Alexander, Mason).

From the very beginning the growing ego begins to form some
introject (pre-object; part object), though before three months it is
scarcely noticeable. Slowly the introject takes over more and more
of the mental life. Early experience dictates the kind of introject
formed; its overwhelming importance stems from that fact.

In cases of maternal loss or prolonged separation from the mother,
Bowlby has described the sequence of protest-despair-detachment.
When a state of detachment is reached, it is virtually impossible to
bring the individual back to human relationships at a later stage; the
earlier replacement occurs, the more likely it is to succeed.

After three months of age, the growing introject, ego, environmental pressures, and the maturation of instinctual needs interact to
form the human personality. The complexity of the process accounts
for the contradictory results secured in experimental research.

While separation in the first three months leads either to death
or the most severe kinds of emotional-psychosomatic disturbance, in
the next three to six months the reaction to maternal separation or
poor mothering is primarily one of depression (Melanie Klein; Mahler:
autism-symbiosis; Kohut: narcissism). Physiology still plays a predominant role in the first year. In spite of all vicissitudes, normal
development along a variety of lines can be described (Anna Freud).

The unexpected discoveries of the role of human milk and the
great value of breast feeling lend added support to the theory of the
bad breast. De Mause's historical work (1974) shows that in the
course of history the mistreatment of infants has gradually been
ameliorated, lending support to a more optimistic view of human
experience.

Because of physiological limitations genital experience in the first
year plays a minor role. However, it is clear that the nature of early
experience has a decisive effect on later genital experience, when it
becomes physiologically ready to occur (Harlow, Freud).

The father's task in this period is to be of assistance to the mother.
Because of the need to subordinate his other desires to the welfare
of the infant, conflicts frequently arise.

THE ANAL PHASE (ONE TO THREE YEARS)

Developments in the anal phase occur after a considerable period in the oral phase, so that they are bound to be more complex and variable. In this respect, it is to be noted that the early observations on the anal phase and the anal character, while correct as far as they go, are of limited value today because at that time (prior to World War I) it was incorrectly assumed that no regression occurs deeper than the anal, no adequate concept of the ego was available, and there was still insufficient awareness of hostility as an independent drive.

Libidinal Manifestations: Anal Wishes

Libidinally the most obvious feature of this phase is the need to acquire bladder and bowel control. Looking forward, we can already observe that many sexual problems are directly related to unresolved toilet problems. In both sexes the organs of excretion are either the same as or close by the organs of sexual pleasure. Many people are brought up with the idea of sex as a kind of evacuation, as in the commonly heard phrase when the primal scene is first discovered: father pissed into mother's behind. Others are unable to separate the feelings of shame and guilt connected with the toilet from the sexual act. Still others hold on to the sexual pleasure associated with toilet function, e.g., anal pleasure; many girls in particular hold on to extreme pleasure connected with anal play, which they feel obligated to conceal.

Under the influence of Freudian thinking, enlightened pediatricians and educators have recommended that toilet training be deferred until somewhere between the second and third year. When that is done, a frequent experience is that the child, urged to go "pottie" as a form of identification with the parent, takes his training in stride. Normally the toilet training will then leave no significant aftereffects; the child moves on to the tasks of the next stage in development, retaining, however, a variable amount of libidinal gratification in his excretions.

If, however, toilet training is full of conflict, marked consequences on later character formation will ensue. These were well described by Freud and his early collaborators.

Anal Character

One should keep well in mind the two fundamental phases of the process—the first one of "keeping back" and the second one of "giving out," each of which gives rise to its own series of character traits. With both of them the person strongly objects to being thwarted, to being prevented from either "keeping back" or "giving out,'" as the case may be. This attitude may lead to marked individualism, self-will, obstinacy, irritability, and bad temper. Heavy-mindedness, dogged persistence, and concentration, with a passion for thoroughness and completeness, are characteristics equally related to both phases.

Much of the person's later character will depend on the detailed interplay of the attitudes distinctive of each phase, and on the extent to which he may react to each by developing either a positive sublimation or a negative reaction formation. The sublimations result in two contrasting character types: on the one hand a parsimonious and perhaps avaricious one, with a fondness for possessing and caring for objects (collectors), and a great capacity for tenderness so long as the loved person is docile; on the other hand, a more creative and productive type, with active tendencies to imprint the personality on something or somebody, with a fondness for molding and manipulating, and a great capacity for giving, especially in love. The reaction formations lead to the character traits of orderliness, cleanliness, pedantry, with a dislike of waste; they also afford important contributions to aesthetic tendencies.

Erikson (1950) describes the conflict at this stage as one of autonomy vs. shame and doubt, as contrasted with that of the oral stage, where the problem is to acquire a basic trust in other people. Generally bowel training is the first severe demand for control which the parent makes on the child. Since such a demand is not easy, even if it comes relatively late, conflicts are bound to ensue. The outcome of these conflicts will determine whether the child will be obstinate, defiant, rebellious, self-willed, and hostile to authority, or compliant, cooperative, and willing to play ball with authority. Reactions to the first authority figures, the parents, will as a rule carry over to other authority figures, although many exceptions are noted.

Language

A second profound change in the anal phase occurs with the development of language. Ordinarily the child begins to speak a few words toward the end of the first year, after which speech and language growth proceed continuously as part of the maturation of the cognitive processes.

Too little attention has been paid to the role of language in the whole maturation process. This topic will be discussed in more detail in Chapter 9. Here our concern is mainly with the way the onset and growth of language are related ultimately to the nature of the individual's sexual adjustment.

Language, although its growth shows certain similarities in all people which point to innate constitutional factors (Chomsky, 1968), is after all a form of communication. Once meaningful words and sentences can be formed, the gesture language of infancy which formerly prevailed can slowly be abandoned or outgrown. Thus the linguistic capacity of the child becomes one measure of its relatedness to other people.

The capacity to communicate with others via language becomes a measure of the individual's ability to outgrow the ties to the mother, enter into peer relationships, and handle life's problems on a more mature level. Consequently any inhibition in linguistic development must have repercussions on the libidinal interchange.

Growth to Father

The growth process may be formulated as moving from mother to father to the outside world. In the anal phase the first steps toward father are taken. One immediate consequence is that the child first becomes aware of homosexual impulses by noticing the differences between the sexes. At this point the child is still very much tied to the parent's body. Cuddling, caressing, playing, piggy-back rides, tickling, kissing, and many other forms of bodily contact are perfectly acceptable, as a rule even encouraged, not only with the father but with many other adults as well.

The homosexuality of this phase must be considered normal, in that it is an outgrowth of the wish to play with the big warm body of the parent. If, however, as is so often the case, the parents have their own conflicts about being played with it can become a source of considerable conflict. The genesis of adult homosexuality is seen in the fixation on the mother, but if the father rejects the child's attention to his body, at this stage especially the child is almost forcibly thrown back on the mother.

Bisexuality

Inability to master the homosexual conflict at this point leads to a marked bisexuality, usually at an unconscious level, which likewise interferes with later sexual adjustment. Right before puberty there is another upsurge of homosexual feeling, which must likewise be overcome to allow heterosexual pleasure. The outcome of this conflict at puberty would depend on the management of the earlier conflict in the anal period.

Hostility

Because the child now begins to walk and move about more freely, the nature of the conflicts surrounding hostility begins to change. For the first time hostility can take a directly aggressive form in which other people can be hurt, at times quite seriously. Often younger children or playmates are the butts of the aggression, and the mother or other adults must come to their defense. Many of the inner conflicts surrounding sadism described by Melanie Klein seem more appropriately placed here than in the oral stage. Anal sadism can come out in a wide variety of fantasies, and occasionally actions. Regression to anal sadism in many forms of adult sex play is quite common.

Because hostility now has noticeable undesirable consequences, its management now takes an entirely different turn. The child must learn that if he hits he may be hit back, and that frequently this will hurt. While children of this age are often seemingly oblivious of the hurt, many others become excessively frightened. They may cling to mother's skirts rather than pursue a fight. Size and innate physical ability begin to play a role.

Dependency and Attachment

Dependency and attachment needs naturally diminish only gradually. By the age of two, sometimes much earlier, the symbiotic and autistic modes of relating are already well defined and easily observed. The separation-individuation process has started, and is resolved in varying degrees in different activities. Any disturbance in this area again becomes a forerunner of later disturbances in genitality.

Four aspects of motility are of special psychological interest in infants and children: (a) affectomotor patterns; (b) vigorous rhythmic patterns, usually referred to as autoerotic; (c) skilled motor activities; and (d) motor phenomena that are indispensable elements in the function of other organs (Mittelmann, 1954). The further development of these aspects and their interaction with other components of the ego structure can be traced.

Sibling Rivalry

Sibling rivalry is almost universal in this period when there is a sibling. Whether this is an artifact of Western culture, or inherent in all family structures, is hard to say. Certainly it seems difficult to avoid jealousy reactions.

"Partial Instincts"

Finally a word should be said about the component or *partial instincts* that Freud had originally posited in his 1905 work to explain many of the varieties of sexual response. Once a structural theory is adopted, as at present, and hostility is seen as an independent drive, there seems to be no need to classify these as instincts. Sadism and masochism refer to the interaction of hostility with sexuality. Exhibitionism and voyeurism refer to bodily and self-image gratification within the family structure, later outside. No special hypotheses are needed to explain their dynamics.

THE PHALLIC PHASE (THREE TO FIVE YEARS)

As with the anal phase, the phallic phase follows a long developmental process. Accordingly its manifestations, while uniform in a certain general way, will display many more variations because of the numerous differences in the earlier history.

Further, many aspects of development are found here which are not directly related to sexuality. Ego, superego growth, language, symbolism, motor growth, and many other personality features could be described, but would take us too far afield. Their fuller discussion will be deferred until appropriate chapters later. In this section the focus will be squarely on the libidinal manifestations and the early love experiences.

The outstanding new feature of this period is the conscious search for pleasure in the genitals. There is nothing in the sexual apparatus itself to account for this; it is rather an outgrowth of the entire maturation process.

Incest and Incest Taboo

Inasmuch as the nuclear family is universal (Murdock, 1949), the easiest partner is the parent of the opposite sex. Against such a choice the powerful taboo of incest has been set up by all known societies, one of the strongest of all taboos. Incest, its folklore, and its psychology thus become some of the central topics in the understanding of the human being.

Oedipus Complex

The incest taboo becomes institutionalized through the Oedipus complex. In the original Greek play the hero, without knowing it, commits the unpardonable sin of marrying his mother, and the somewhat less unpardonable one of murdering his father; for these crimes he pays the inevitable price. Oedipus' "ignorance" of what he has done has been interpreted as a Greek way of describing his unconscious.

The Oedipal conflict may be viewed as a natural result of the growth of the child. Initially relating only to the mother, he then moves on to the father, thereby entering a triangle situation. In this triangle, then, a natural wish makes itself felt, to take the father's place and do to the mother what the father has done to her. A parallel process takes place with girls.

Universality of Oedipus Conflicts

By now the evidence seems clear that the Oedipus conflict is to be found in all human beings, in all cultures. In this respect it may be noted that the widely diffused statement that Malinowski "refuted" the universality of the Oedipus complex by showing that the Trobriand Islanders put the maternal uncle in the same place as the father in our culture rests on an incorrect interpretation of the Polish-English anthropologist. What Malinowski actually said was (1923, p. 431):

> By my analysis, I have established that Freud's theories not only roughly correspond to human psychology, but that they follow closely the modifications in human nature brought about by various constitutions of Society. In other words, I have established a deep correlation between the type of society and the nuclear complex found there. While this is a notable confirmation of the main tenet of Freudian psychology, it might compel us to modify certain of its details, or rather to make some of the formulae more elastic.

It is the Oedipal situation that explains the emotional needs that are served by the family, likewise a universal human institution. Incidentally, it is worth noting at this point that research has shown that the nuclear family has been far more common historically than had previously been thought (Laslett, ed., 1972).

Sexual Curiosity and Fantasies

Within our cultural framework, once the Oedipus complex is reached, the child begins to wonder about sexuality and its many ramifications. When he is not told the truth, still usually the case, he engages in sexual researches that lead to a variety of persistent and damaging fantasies. Though there are certain similarities, the fantasies are markedly different in the two sexes.

Childhood Masturbation

The major physical sexual outlet in this period is masturbation. There is no evidence considered reliable today that masturbation is in any degree harmful to the individual, whether child or adult. However, it has taken a long time to reach such an enlightened position. Large segments of the population are still convinced that masturbation will drive them crazy or send them straight to hell. Consequently the guilt attached to masturbation is still an important psychological factor in our current civilization.

Childhood Sex Play

With regard to other forms of sex play in the Oedipal period, physical contact with the parents is quite commonly found, but usually with avoidance of the genitals, insofar as that is possible. More often there is a denial of the emotional significance of genital contact. Ford and Beach (1951, p. 197) find that as long as the adult members of a society permit them to do so, immature males and females engage in practically every type of sexual behavior found in grown men and women. Nor is there any evidence of harmful consequences deriving from any of these sexual practices, horrifying though they may be to a puritanical Westerner.

THE LATENCY PERIOD (SIX YEARS TO PUBERTY)

The Oedipal period is resolved by the formation of a superego (internalization of the parents), identifications with the parent fig--ures, abandonment of the earlier desires for incestuous gratifications, and involvement in a first love affair. During this period sexual manifestations tend to be minimal or quiescent.

It is by now generally agreed that the latency period has both biological and cultural determinants. Biologically, the child now becomes more interested in his ego and superego consolidation and growth potential, so that the body and mind are both available for far more than sexual gratification per se. Culturally the degree of withdrawal from sexual preoccupation depends very heavily on the whole sexual climate of the culture, as Freud had observed; Róheim (1932) in fact denied that any latency period at all existed in the group that he studied. Conflicting opinions can be found about the degree to which a real latency period can be uncovered in our contemporary civilization. In the light of the many different attitudes toward sexuality expressed in various cultural groups, it seems inevitable that the absence or presence of sexual activity in latency would vary widely. Statistics for this are hard to come by, even if their meaning could be deciphered.

THE FIRST LOVE AFFAIR (SIX OR SEVEN)

Internally the Oedipus complex is outgrown by the formation of a superego and identification with the parent. Externally, however, another important stage occurs here, in the child's first love affair. It seems to be true in general that the human being cannot give up an important person except by the substitution of another important person. From mother the child moves to father. From father the child moves on to another child, with whom a love relationship similar to or in imitation of what they see in their parents is set up.

This first love may occur anywhere from five to ten, but it is more often seen at the early stage than at the later one. In some cases it is entirely absent. But when it is absent, the child has not succeeded in liberating itself from its parents, the consequences of which are dire indeed for later personality formation. This is one of the roots of a later schizophrenic development.

BROTHER-SISTER CONFLICT: AVOIDANCE AND EXTRUSION

Even though the changes are much less noticeable to the child and the adult than those that occur later, at puberty proper, virtually all societies have found themselves constrained to adopt new measures for the social regulation of children at this age (eight to ten). Yehudi Cohen (1966) has summarized the evidence from many cultures which shows that the greatest danger feared at this time is brother-sister incest, and accordingly measures have to be taken to keep brother and sister apart. The two institutionalized customs are extrusion and brother-sister avoidance.

PEER GROUPS

It is at this age too that the child (eight years on) becomes ready for peer groups, which begin to form. Such groups as the Boy Scouts, secret societies, clubs, gangs, and the like serve a variety of inner needs, one of which is the regulation of the brother-sister attachment: by removing the child from the immediate threat he is helped in his growth process, whereas if there were no such institutions, the fixations on brother or sister could easily become too great. Clinically, it can readily be observed that the children who do not engage in these peer-group activities remain undesirably fixated on either the parents or the siblings.

PREADOLESCENT SEXUALITY (AGES ELEVEN TO PUBERTY)

After the first stage of puberty, or the precursor of puberty, whichever name one wishes to use, there is a transition to a homosexual period, in which the strongest libidinal attachment is to a member of the same sex, usually of the same age, but often an older man or woman, in many cases a substitute parent figure. Ford and Beach (1951), in their summary of anthropological and biological data, conclude that there is a biological tendency for sexual inversion inherent in most if not all mammals, including the human species. At the same time homosexuality is never the predominant type of sexual activity for adults in any society or in any animal species.

PARENTAL IDENTIFICATION

There is also a strong desire for emulation of the strong parent of the same sex at this point. The boy adores his father, the girl her mother. In other cultures, such as ancient Greece, the idea that an older man should initiate a boy of this age into the mysteries of life was accepted as a natural one (Licht, 1932). The same is true in many other cultures. Unable to reach the parent, the boy or girl does the next best thing, and picks a slightly older playmate.

SUMMARY COMMENTS

Freud's division of the sexual instinct into an object and an aim, the development of each of which could be traced independently, was a stroke of genius. Using his scheme as an outline, one could trace the course of the sexual aim as follows: oral, anal, phallic, genital.

Less obvious but even more important in its ultimate effects is the development of the sexual object. This runs in our culture from mother to father to first love affair to sibling to homosexual companion to heterosexual object. Most significant is the fact that the human being is so strongly atttached to people that they assume overpowering meaning for him, and cannot easily be given up. In fact, they can be given up only by an attachment to another person. This shift from one attachment to another is a complex process before puberty. Should there be a failure at any stage, which is more the rule than the exception, the individual's capacity to make a satisfactory heterosexual adjustment at puberty may be severely damaged.

Despite the diversity of mores and practices, human sexuality seems basically the same the world over. Virtually all humans share a sexual drive that generally becomes strongly operant around puberty, although it often develops before then. After childhood and an early adolescent phase of masturbation and sociosexual experimentation, most individuals make heterosexual coitus their chief sexual activity. Such coitus ultimately involves a strong affectional relationship in many cases, and this culminates in marriage. However, marriage does not suffice to satisfy the emotional needs and sexual needs of a substantial proportion of persons; and extramarital coitus, sanctioned or not, is not uncommon. Also there seems to be a basic similarity among humans in physiological response to sexual stimuli and in psychological reactions. All persons are kin in sharing much the same interests, lusts, frustrations, loves, sorrows, and joys that are part of human sexuality.

Historically, Freud's achievement lay in uncovering the nature of the sexual psychosis that has beset Western man for two thousand years, in proposing a scheme for normal development, and in showing that later sexual disturbance derives from earlier frustration with the parents. Though widely touted, neither the Kinsey report nor the Masters-Johnson studies affect the major psychoanalytic theses; in essence they tend to confirm them (Fine, 1971). The anthropological data indicate that the basic physiological drive is so strong that it tends to override cultural restrictions. What results, however, is an enormous amount of guilt and unhappiness.

For normal sexual development it is essential to stress the prototype of satisfaction as seen in the first year of life: a balance between gratification by others and self-gratification. This balance must be handled differently at different ages in the individual's life, and must be brought in line with many other elements in the psyche. Theory fights shy of attractive oversimplifications. However, the concept of balance and the biological rhythm described above remain basic.

CHAPTER 6

Anxiety and Hostility

The other two instinctual feelings are anxiety and hostility (as will be indicated, this term is more precise than aggression). Where one exists, the other can be found as well. The difference becomes mainly one of conscious experience, as well as of emphasis. Actually, both enter into the ego structure in such a detailed way that they are basically inferences from the data, rather than direct observation. Still, for clarity, it is necessary to handle them separately.

ANXIETY

The vast amount of data on anxiety can best be ordered in accordance with the metapsychological approach described in Chapter 1.

1. *Topographically,* unconscious anxiety turns out to be as important as conscious anxiety. In fact, because anxiety is so subjectively painful, it tends to become pushed into the unconscious, from where it continues to exert a powerful influence. Paradoxically, the capacity to tolerate conscious anxiety indicates a stronger ego than its absence.

2. *Genetically,* anxiety must be considered in relation to the weakness of the ego and the development of the object. Spitz (1965) enumerates three phases in the development of the object: (a) the pre-objectal or objectless stage (to three months); (b) the stage of the precursor of the object (three to eight months); (c) the stage of the libidinal object proper (eight months on). It is only in this third stage, he argues, that one can speak of anxiety about separation from the mother, for it is only then that the infant has matured enough to be aware of her comings and goings. This has become known as the

eight-month anxiety, although other authors variously place it any-where from three months to one year.

In normal development, the infant moves toward a state of object constancy, in which the internal representative of the caretaker (mo-ther, essentially, in our culture) remains constant even in her absence. Mahler (1968) places this at three years; other authors earlier. As the object becomes increasingly internalized, anxiety regulation moves more and more toward the internal rather than the external source.

Consequently, separation from this internal source (introject, later superego) is always difficult. In fact, such separation always involves some intermediate object, usually a person. The human being appar-ently cannot leave one attachment figure without having another available. The only apparent exception is the "transitional object" described by Winnicott (1953), although there too the role of the father remains obscure.

In the earliest stages, separation from the mother arouses anxiety of the most intense kind, eventually leading to a state of detachment (Bowlby). In this state the infant has given up all hope of ever deriving gratification from other human beings. Detachment follows upon protest and despair.

Bowlby's paradigm is similar to Selye's (1956) three stages in the *general adaptation syndrome* (GAS): alarm, resistance, resignation. Spitz also draws many parallels between his *emotional deprivation syndrome* (EDS) and Selye's GAS.

GAS (SELYE)	EDS (SPITZ)
Tension	Weepiness
Excitement	Demanding appetite
Loss of Appetite	Loss of appetite
	Loss of weight
Resistance to evocative stimulus in-creases	Social sector increases
Adaptability to other agents diminishes	Arrest and regression of D.Q. (devel-
Libido subnormal	opmental quotient)
Depression of nervous system	
Adaptation stops	Absence of autoerotic activity
Resistance ceases	Withdrawal
Arteriosclerosis of brain vessels	Insomnia
Breakdown	Decreased motility
Death	Regression of D.Q. irreversible
	Infection liability
	Facial rigidity
	Atypical finger movements
	Morbidity increases
	Spectacular mortality

Thus there is available here from an integration of material from many sources a unitary conception of the matrix from which psychotic, neurotic, and psychosomatic disorders grow. The infant that lives is left in a state of restlessness, anxiety, bodily weakness, and a general susceptibility to psychosomatic disorders.

As the individual grows, anxiety is handled in accordance with the ego structure developed.

3. *Dynamically*, anxiety is so intolerable that defenses against it are set up to prevent it from becoming conscious. This is the core of the defensive ego, which likewise grows gradually. The greater the anxiety, the more pathological the defense. Hence it is conceptualized (Sullivan) that the schizophrenic suffers from panic states similar to the earliest anxieties, and because of the weakness of his ego defends against these panic states in a variety of bizarre ways which account for the peculiarity of the symptomatology. Since anxiety and defenses occur in everybody, a continuum theory of emotional disturbance which assumes that "all human beings are more simply human than otherwise" (Sullivan) seems justified, rather than a theory that separates out the mentally ill as biological freaks.

4. *Economically*, anxiety may be free-floating or bound (phobia).

5. *Structurally*, Freud moved from his first theory of anxiety, that it is a toxicological transformation of sexuality, to the second, separation anxiety, a signal emitted by the ego to warn of danger. Since the major danger signal is the disapproval of the parents, it could just as well be argued that anxiety comes to reside in the superego. This makes most sense in the light of our present knowledge.

Somatically, anxiety has profound consequences. Conceptualized first as the fight-flight syndrome (Cannon), it has since been shown (Selye, Alexander, Mason) that virtually any physiological reaction can be affected by emotion. What is necessary in all cases is to trace a precise chain from the original psychic trauma to the final somatic result. Such chains are the goals of current research, even if they are often elusive with the present state of knowledge.

Two major forms of anxiety can be distinguished: external and internal.

The earliest forms of anxiety are felt as external threats, hence separation, on the one hand, or damage (paranoid) on the other. Later, as the ego develops, these become more internalized, and are felt as depression (loss of love) and castration (loss of capacity for pleasure). The child's tendency is to see all danger as coming from the outside; it is only with the growth of the ego that the awareness of internal danger comes to consciousness. Psychoanalysis involves the translation of externally perceived anxieties into internal ones.

6. *Culturally,* cultural pressures, first through the parents, later through the superego, sanction certain kinds of fears as acceptable or communicable, while they condemn other kinds. Thus the individual personality is always most deeply responsive to cultural rewards and punishments.

Second, and equally important, the culture has to provide the life environment that will make the individual feel more or less secure. Since theoretical work has reached the conclusion that these culturally induced insecurities are of vital importance in the mental health of the individual, a different attitude toward the culture has been emerging.

7. *Interpersonally,* anxiety is aroused by other people, and often assuaged by other people (cf. Fenichel's remarks about the schizophrenic as an "object addict"). It is an exquisitely interpersonal phenomenon, even though it has far-reaching intrapersonal consequences. However, it is not the other person as such, but his psychic representative, which is often quite distorted.

Inasmuch as all anxieties come from or derive from the parents, a study of the family is fundamental to its understanding. Basic security is built up with the parents, first with mother, later with father. This topic then merges into the whole question of the social structure, which will be taken up in detail later.

8. *Adaptively,* anxiety serves an obvious function, since it helps the person escape serious threat. Only social animals, with an autonomic nervous system, experience anxiety; others may have other weapons (skunk, porcupine, snake, turtle). But apart from these intringuing biological observations, the question of adaptation has no further importance for psychology.

HOSTILITY

In spite of all the literature devoted to it, few subjects in the whole area of psychoanalysis and psychology are so poorly understood as the topic of hostility. As recently as 1973 Arlow (p. 184) could say that "we are thus only at the beginning of our concern" with this central topic.

At the meeting of the International Psychoanalytic Association in 1971, held, appropriately, in Vienna, whose hostility had made Freud an exile at the age of eighty-two, the central theme was aggression. Most of the speakers stressed the disagreements among workers in the field, and the need for clarification.

In what was no doubt the best paper at the Vienna symposium, Charles Brenner (1971, p. 143) sums up available psychoanalytic knowledge about aggression as follows:

> 1. Psychological evidence seems to be an acceptable basis for the concept of aggression as instinctual drive. Supporting evidence from other branches of biology, though it would be welcome, is not essential, nor is it available at present.
>
> 2. No source of aggression can be specified, other than a psychological one. Aggression cannot, at present, be related to any physiological phenomenon other than brain functioning.
>
> 3. There is no evidence at present to support the view that the aggressive drive is a measure of the demand of bodily processes on mental functioning.
>
> 4. Aggression and libido bear similar relations to the pleasure principle. In general, discharge is associated with pleasure; lack of discharge with unpleasure.
>
> 5. The respective roles of the two drives are likewise similar with respect to psychical conflict.
>
> 6. The aim of aggression is not uniformly destruction of the cathected object. On the contrary, the aim is variable and is intimately related to experience and to ego function.
>
> 7. In general, the relationship between ego functions and drives is an extremely complex and close one.
>
> 8. It seems impossible to decide at present between a theory of drive fusion and that of drive differentiation.

DISTINCTION OF "ASSERTIVENESS" AND "HOSTILITY"

For the clarification of the theoretical structure, it is necessary to note first of all that considerable confusion has arisen because of the synonymous use of "aggression" and "hostility." In English as well as in German, "aggression" carries with it the connotations of both assertiveness and hostility; therefore, intuitively, it sometimes seems desirable and sometimes undesirable to equate the two. Most of the time our concern is more with hostility than with assertiveness. Originally, Freud and his colleagues before World War I saw assertiveness as a characteristic of all instinctual drives, and this still makes very good sense. It therefore seems simpler to confine the remainder of the discussion to hostility.

The view has been presented before that hostility can be regarded as a reactive instinct. That means that it has to wait to be aroused, but once aroused, it becomes an exceedingly powerful drive. The biological evidence indicates that it is actually stronger in man than in animals.

Further, no physiological basis for the development of hostility has ever been found, as contrasted with sexuality.

However, while hostility has no known physiological *basis,* it has enormously far-reaching and unexpected physiological *consequences.* It would appear that a great many people, probably the vast majority, live a good part or all of their lives in a state of chronic resentment. This chronic resentment has the same kinds of physiological consequences as chronic anxiety. Long-standing resentment and hostility can do serious damage to the body, including death.

THE NATURE OF HOSTILITY

Hostility therefore should be conceptualized as a reactive instinct, psychosocial in nature, with far-ranging physiological consequences. Three main causes can be adduced for its appearance and persistence: (1) the biological inability of the ego to control it adequately, (2) the insecurities and frustrations of the individual's life, and (3) the hostilities instilled into him by his family and his culture.

At an early stage in life hostility is internalized, there to be incorporated by the introject, later the superego. Thereafter the essential target of the hostility is an internal representation, usually projected outward. This combines with externally determined sources of hostility to make up the total hostility pattern. It follows that hostility can be relieved, but never really gratified, since the internal object after a certain stage in life never changes.

One consequence of this internalization is that a distinction can be drawn between love cultures and hate cultures (see Chapter 2). In one sense the major observation contributed by psychoanalysis is the ubiquity of hostility in our culture, which means Western culture for the past two thousand years. This cultural pressure is so great that few individuals can escape it; hence hatred perpetuates hatred. When not directed outward, hostility is directed inward, where it produces lifelong chronic resentment.

EFFECTS OF RELEASE OF HOSTILITY

The notion that the release of hostility is pleasurable and desirable per se goes back to Freud's early concept of strangulated affect, which was to be abreacted under catharsis. But Freud himself soon discovered that neither catharsis nor abreaction had any long-term or noticeable therapeutic effect. It is obvious that there are many patients, particularly certain types of hysterics, who release vast quantities of rage without getting any pleasure from it. In fact, the release of rage can easily provoke serious somatic consequences in many people, including death. The fact that many people state that they would like to release their rage does not alter the fact that when they actually release it, no real change is effected. What happens is that the individual loses control, but loss of control cannot be equated with pleasure (see Chapter 3).

NEUTRALIZATION OF HOSTILITY

In his later writings, Hartmann (1964) appeared to be placing the neutralization of hostility in as central a role as that in which the sublimation of sexuality was placed by Freud in the early part of the century. In terms of total ego and superego functioning, this does not seem to be the case. Certainly the shift from an instinctual mode of discharge to a noninstinctual one is adopted by many people and becomes a permanent part of the ego and superego. It is, however, by no means the only solution, nor is it the solution that is attempted in the process of psychoanalysis. Ideally, as has been pointed out, it is the severity of the superego that must be reduced, as a result of which hostility can no longer be aroused in the same way or with the same effects.

Furthermore, the concept of neutralization suffers from essentially the same objection as the concept of sublimation: that it is tied to some socially approved goal, which may or may not be considered desirable. In addition, the neutralization concept appears to rest upon the separation of hostility from its sources of formation, thereby shifting from an attack on these sources (frustrations, culture) to a manipulation of the reaction.

HOSTILITY AND RATIONALIZATION

A word should be said about the universal tendency to rationalization of the hostile impulse. Since in adult life it is directed against the superego, to acknowledge hostility means to incur the wrath of the superego, genetically the wrath of the parents, which is much too frightening. This would also explain the fear of retaliation for any hostile action—unconsciously the retaliation is the retaliation of the parents, which could be totally destructive to the child. It would also explain why the effects of hostility are so often overrated by the individual. None of this applies to anxiety, which thus is further differentiated intrapsychically from hostility by these considerations.

HOSTILITY AND HAPPINESS

Apart from variability, and the consistency found in any culture, the question can be raised as to whether the people in various cultures are happy or not, and if so to what degree. The analytic proposition that a surplus of hostility and violence makes for unhappiness, while an atmosphere of security and nonviolence makes for happiness, seems to be borne out by the study of other cultures.

INTEGRATION

Hostility is to be looked upon as a reactive instinct. It is essentially a psychosocial drive, with biological roots and far-reaching physiological consequences. It may be said to have three basic causes: (a) the biological basis of the human being, (b) frustration, and (c) socialization, especially early childhood experiences. Of these three, for theoretical and remedial purposes, b, the frustration-aggression hypothesis, is the most relevant.

CHAPTER 7

Dreams and the Unconscious

Just as the investigation of perception and the cognitive processes has been the hallmark of academic and experimental psychology, the investigation of the dream and fantasy processes has been the province of clinical psychology. There is now substantial evidence that the dream is of such vital importance that its study sheds an illuminating light on all human experience. The dream is the most exquisitely human of all psychological productions; it provides clues to human functioning that can be found either nowhere else, or not as clearly anywere else. Truly, as Shakespeare put it, we are "the stuff that dreams are made on."

FREUD'S INTERPRETATION OF DREAMS

The book in which the theory of the dream was formulated was Freud's *The Interpretation of Dreams* (1900), universally regarded as his greatest work. It is indeed a monumental achievement, which has stood the test of time well. It can rightly be viewed as one of the classics of all scientific literature.

Freud's theory is elegant in its simplicity. The dream represents the royal road to the unconscious. Its essence is that it allows the individual to fantasize wishes that are ordinarily barred from consciousness; the consequent distortion of these wishes accounts for the apparent absurdity or bizarreness of the dream. What appears on the surface is the *manifest content;* through associations to this material we get to the *latent content,* the true dream. The pathway from the latent to the manifest content is known as the dream work. In a dream the individual regresses to childhood, which explains why the dream is so heavily visual in content and devoid of abstract ideas. The dream takes off from a seemingly trivial or indifferent event in the previous twenty-four hours, known as the *day residue* (Fisher has extended this to seventy-two hours). The wishes involved, initially seen as sexual, are now regarded as any manifestation of the id.

In the dream, the ego is weak, while the superego appears as a punishing force. Thus the structure of the dream, once unraveled, is this: a wish, transformed by the basic mechanisms of condensation, displacement, and symbolization, and taking as its starting point some event of the most recent past (24 to 72 hours), is first gratified and then punished or thwarted in some way. Children often have dreams that embody simple wish-fulfillment, in which punishment is absent; adults rarely do. The healthier the individual becomes, the less punishment he will experience in his dreams.

Two processes operate in the mind: primary and secondary. In the primary process there is nothing but wishing, leading to mobile cathexes and a pressure for discharge. The secondary process is that of reason, or the ego, which molds these wishes into a form ultimately acceptable to the superego.

There are typical dreams, the elucidation of which requires no associations. These correspond to the universal fantasies of mankind, and are found in similar form in all cultures.

Both the remembering and forgetting of dreams are unconsciously determined. By and large dreams are frightening to people in our culture, and are therefore remembered mainly when someone offers support, as in therapy or research.

DREAMS AND PERSONALITY STRUCTURE

Freud's theory of dreams is obviously more than just a speculation about dreams; it is a highly articulated, deeply thought-through theory of human functioning, which has become the basis for all dynamic psychology. Its bases, however, were spelled out by Freud more in economic terms than in dynamic, in view of his constant preoccupation, as has now appeared, especially since the posthumous discovery of the *Project for a Scientific Psychology* (Fine, 1973b), with providing some kind of adequate physiological basis for his psychological findings. But it is the dynamic approach that is the great thing in Freud, not the economic. Accordingly it is useful to spell out here the major assumptions of his dynamic theory of personality, as it appeared then, with whatever changes seem appropriate now.

1. *Fantasy productions are highly meaningful.* The dream per se is only the most pronounced of all the fantasy materials that the human being produces. But on the basis of Freud's dream studies, psychoanalysts and other dynamically oriented professionals began to examine other kinds of fantasy productions, using the same principles that Freud had used for the dream. The results of these studies have led to a great extension of psychological knowledge.

2. *The production and organization of fantasies are guided by underlying wishes.* These wishes are inferred from the content of the fantasies; the methods of inference are essentially similar to what Freud did with the dream. The prime requisite for accurate inference is to get the associations of the fantasizer; when these are absent, the result is less cogent. However, as with typical dreams, there are many situations where the fantasy can be corrently interpreted even without associations.

3. *The wishes are closely related to, if not directly derived from, instinctual feelings.* Thus fantasies never really get too far away from the basic needs and desires of the person. This means that they are not spun out of the blue, but have some deep meaning for the person.

4. *Both ego and id operate in the production of fantasies, in varying degrees.* In the dream the id appears in purer form than in any other fantasy production, although ego factors play a role as well (E. Hartmann, ed., 1970). Social factors will also play a part in the respective roles of each of the two psychic instances; thus it has been noted that in the religions of primitive peoples, the id elements are preponderant, while as one goes up the social ladder the ego becomes stronger.

5. *The wishes are related to childhood experiences.* Just as the dream is a "piece of mental life that has been superseded," so are all fantasies. There is even some physiological basis for the psychological observation that children's fantasies are stronger, more persistent, and more important than adults'. Further, men live in their memories, and much of what they do is the result of a variety of remembered experiences.

6. *Conscious productions are a clue to unconscious forces.* This can be put in various ways. Consciousness is like a sense organ that selec-

tively allows material that is least anxiety-provoking to sift through; consciousness determines which aspects of the unconscious will break through to it. Studies of nonrecallers of dreams suggest that they forget their dreams because of the anxiety they are apt to arouse (E. Hartmann, ed., 1970).

Freud's assumption of a preconscious goes back to his three types of neurones posited in the *Project for a Scientific Psychology*. It is redundant, however, and the concept of a preconscious can be eliminated without any loss of adequacy of explanation or scientific rigor.

7. *Percept and fantasy are reciprocally inhibiting.* Perception interferes with the fantasy life; hence whenever anyone wishes to elicit fantasies, all that has to be done is to reduce or eliminate perceptual cues. This applies to dreams, of course; sleep per se is possible only when all perceptual stimuli are eliminated. Contrariwise, fantasizing is interfered with by any perceptual activity.

8. *The mind is always active: either it perceives or it fantasizes.* Apparently the mind is never completely quiescent, a fact that has baffled sleep researchers, who had hoped to find some period in which there is a total absence of brain activity. But there is only relative quiescence, never absolute. Even though NREM sleep is relatively more quiescent than REM sleep, even during NREM time there are some dreams, and when the person is awakened he reports some kind of mental activity. Thus the waking-sleep cycle is paralleled by a percept-fantasy cycle, with differing emphases on each part in different people.

9. *Behavior cannot be properly understood without knowing the underlying fantasy on which it is based.* No piece of external behavior is fully comprehensible in its own terms; it must always be related to the underlying fantasies that describe its meaning to the individual. True enough, one can direct or alter or modify behavior without knowing what the fantasies are, but that is entirely different from understanding. For a complete comprehension of the human being, a knowledge of his inner fantasies is indispensable.

10. *External forces may set off fantasies, but internal factors determine how the person will react to them.* This gets us back to the fundamental formula $R = f(P,S)$. In dreams this is completely obvious, since it can easily be demonstrated experimentally that the same stimulus will lead to different dreams in different people. This principle becomes the basis for the *projective techniques*. There the perceptual cues are minimized by making the stimulus or stimulus situation ambiguous.

Such is the foundation of the house that Freud built. If one were to ask what the scientific evidence is for such a theory, the answer would have to be found in the total body of knowledge available to dynamic psychologists today. The dream is only one.

It is true that this theory as a whole cannot be put to any crucial test, which is why so many psychologists have tended to reject it. But it leads to so many experimental situations that can be put to the test, and it explains so many clinical phenomena that either cannot easily be replicated in experimental paradigms or cannot be replicated at all, that to reject the theory on such grounds is wholly fallacious. Such rejection derives more from a misunderstanding of the nature of scientific method than the reverse (see Chapter 1). In this respect the total psychological dynamic theory outlined here does not differ from such all-encompassing theories as evolution, relativity, or even the theory of gravitation, all of which also involve integration of numerous pieces of evidence, yet none of which can be put to a crucial test per se.

To return to the subject of dreams proper: certain small changes have to be made in Freud's theory as presented above, none of them of decisive consequence. Instead of the censor we would have to write the superego. The image of the mind would have to be recast in cybernetic or computer-style language. Anxiety dreams could be explained more readily by the mechanism of the superego, though the transformation of libido into anxiety on a psychological (not physiological) basis could still be maintained. That the dream is the guardian of sleep could be questioned, though it is beyond question that some dreams sometimes help the dreamer sleep by offering him sufficient gratification, while at other times some dreams wake the dreamer because they are too frightening. At still other times insomnia or hypersomnia can both be related to the dreaming process. But apart from these and perhaps a few other changes, Freud's theory stands intact. What has followed has taken the form of additions and confirmations rather than of changes in the basic structure.

THE DREAM-SLEEP CYCLE: *REM* SLEEP

At first sight sleep and the dream-sleep cycle look like a purely physiological phenomenon. Such a view was completely shattered by the serendipitous discovery of Aserinsky and Kleitman in 1953 that eye movements during sleep were signs that the subject was dreaming. This was expanded to the finding that there are regularly recurring periods of sleep which are physiologically different from the rest, showing a characteristic EEG pattern together with bursts of bilaterally · synchronous, conjugate, rapid vertical and horizontal eye movements, and that this whole pattern was highly correlated with dream recall. The sleep period was then subdivided into REM (rapid eye movements) and NREM (non-rapid eye movements). This led to the development of an EEG-REM monitoring technique, an objective method applicable to experimental subjects, which opened up many areas hitherto inaccesible to investigation. An excellent summary of the results of these investigations is available in C. Fisher (1965).

THE EXTENT OF DREAMING

One of the most striking findings has been the large amount of dreaming universally present. The normal young adult spends from one-fifth to one-fourth of a seven- to eight-hour sleep period in dreaming. This confirms the conclusion, already suggested by psychoanalytic work, that the mind is never entirely at rest, even in sleep. There is more physiological quiescence during NREM sleep than during REM, but even then some mental activity is going on. REMs never occur at sleep onset, but only after a prolonged period of NREM, pointing to an alternation of greater and lesser quiescence (this is similar to the physiological cycle of need-gratification-rest-need described earlier, and it is also to be noted that REM periods are almost always accompanied by sexual fantasies, as seen in the penis erections).

CYCLIC PERIODICITY OF ERECTION

A finding of major importance is that there is a cyclic periodicity of erection in sleep. This was reported in the forties, but no attention was paid to it until Fisher also demonstrated that the erections coincide with the REM periods, thus tending to confirm Freud's hypothesis that most dreams are centered around sexual wishes. Incidentally, this would also tend to confirm the revised theory of instincts put forth in the present volume, since it once more shows that sexual drives can arise spontaneously and do arise spontaneously, while hostile-anxious feelings are reactive.

TRAUMATIC DREAMS AND NIGHTMARES

More light has been shed on the topic of traumatic dreams and nightmares by a later study of Fisher's (Fisher et al., 1970). The methodology here was somewhat closer to a clinical one. Newspaper advertisements were placed soliciting people who had nightmare experiences. After an initial psychiatric interview, thirty-eight subjects who reported having frequent nightmares, three or more per week, were selected for investigation. These thirty-eight subjects were studied for a total of 162 nights, ranging from one to twenty-three. The procedure was to allow the subject to sleep undisturbed until he had a spontaneous awakening associated with anxiety. He was then interviewed through an intercom in an attempt to elicit content. With some subjects who developed stage 4 nightmares, awakenings were made during subsequent REM periods in order to elicit dream content. Careful note was made of all verbalizations, vocalizations, and other aspects of the sleep behavior or the subjects on a sleep chart.

Fisher's main conclusion was that the nightmare represents a failure of the ego to control anxiety. His group also demonstrated unequivocally that the majority of the pathological manifestations of sleep—sleepwalking, most sleep talking, enuresis, bruxism, the night terror (*pavor nocturnus*) of children and adults—are not associated with dreaming, as has been generally assumed, if dreaming is defined as mental activity during REM periods, but occur during NREM periods.

THE UNCONSCIOUS AND CONSCIOUSNESS

The phenomenon of the dream alone would be sufficient to impress one with the significance of the unconscious. There is, however, much else that leads to the principle that the proper understanding and elucidation of unconscious phenomena are an essential aspect of psychological science.

DESCRIPTIVE AND DYNAMIC UNCONSCIOUS

The term "unconscious" is used in two senses: descriptive and dynamic. The descriptive unconscious refers to the fact that much of what the human being knows is not in the conscious realm. This merely serves to describe the structure of the mental apparatus. For example, any educated person knows how to spell a large number of words, but such knowledge is relegated to another portion of the mind in everyday life, yet readily accessible when needed. This has led to the modern concept of storage and retrieval as the basic paradigm for understanding the descriptive unconscious. From the point of view of the descriptive unconscious, consciousness merely represents the capacity of the mind to pay attention to what is going on, strictly limited by purely mechanical considerations. Thus it is commonly stated that the human being is capable of apprehending seven but not more than seven discrete objects at any one time. Ordinary psychological tests furnish a good categorization of the contents of the descriptive unconscious. The descriptive unconscious and its manifestations form part of the autonomous ego.

The dynamic unconscious, with which psychoanalysis is ordinarily associated, is of an entirely different order. Here material is pushed back or *repressed* into the unconscious because if admitted to consciousness it would arouse too much anxiety. To some extent it depends on brain capacity, like the descriptive unconscious, since the newborn infant can scarcely be expected to comprehend much of what is going on. With the development of the ego, consciousness also develops. However, what is not apprehended for purely neurological reasons has no long-term effect on the individual, whereas what is repressed for psychological reasons (avoidance of anxiety) does. It is only the continuation of operation of repressed material and motives that makes the dynamic unconscious so important.

While both forms of the unconscious are important for a total science of psychology, I shall follow the usual custom here and refer to the dynamic unconscious as the unconscious; when "dynamic" is also intended it will be mentioned specifically. From the viewpoint of the dynamic unconscious, consciousness becomes a kind af sense organ that selectively determines what will be permitted to fiilter through and what will not. By reversing this filtering process some notion can be obtained of what is going on in the unconscious.

CONSCIOUSNESS AND MENTAL HEALTH

From the point of view of the analytic ideal, consciousness represents the state of normality, while the unconscious becomes the touchstone of mental illness. In principle, the greater the degree of consciousness, the healthier the person is. Hence, psychotherapy becomes a process of making the unconscious conscious.

ALTERED STATES OF CONSCIOUSNESS (ASCS)

One of the main characteristics of consciousness is its variability. One major form of variability is sleep, now understood as the dream-sleep cycle. But other ways of altering consciousness have attracted a good deal of attention. In the chapter on pleasure it was seen over and over that the goal of the individual is to change his state of consciousness, rather than to increase his pleasure as such. Therapeutic claims have been put forth for every form of consciousness alteration.

The most important methods of inducing ASCs are (1) sleep, (2) hypnosis, (3) meditation, (4) drugs, (5) sensory deprivation, (6) brain damage, and last but by no means least (7) psychoanalysis.

Psychoanalysis attempts to alter consciousness by a minute and detailed examination of everything that is on the conscious mind, i.e., the free associations. Such meticulous examination will, in the long run, lead to a radically different frame of mind. Further, a large number of studies show that psychoanalysis has marked effects on various of the bodily functions, and exerts a permanent and lasting effect on them. These functions include the many autonomic reactions, such as heart rate, gastric motility and acidity, and brain waves, which adherents of meditative and biofeedback schools claim as their own provinces.

The changes brought about by psychoanalysis are an organic continuation of the main life style of the individual. They differ from changes brought about by other methods in several ways:

1. In psychoanalysis the conscious productions are used to understand the unconscious roots, rather than manipulated.

2. The subject never relinquishes conscious control, or submits without restriction to some higher authority.

3. The changes require long intensive collaborative effort with a trained person, usually lasting over a period of years.

4. The changes are fitted satisfactorily into a total life style, not insinuated bit by bit without reference to the whole life of the individual.

5. The changes make sense in terms of a total psychological structure that explains the conscious mental and somatic phenomena in terms of unconscious mental processes.

6. The changes brought about are by and large more permanent than those produced by any other approach.

CHAPTER 8

Ego Structure

THE ROLE OF REASON IN HUMAN BEHAVIOR

Aristotle's dictum that "man is a rational animal" has dominated the thinking of psychology for the last two thousand years. At the same time, it is quite obvious that man, in many areas of his living, is quite irrational. The resolution of this contradiction is one of the major problems of psychological theory. It may be anticipated, incidentally, that psychoanalytic psychology, which has stressed the irrational elements in man, in its theoretical approach has discovered that all human behavior is rational at an unconscious level. Irrationality consists of the conscious presentation, not of the unconscious ordering.

The questions that theory must answer are these:

1. How is rational thought possible in an organism dominated by feelings, wishes, and desires?
2. What is the relation of reason to these wishes?
3. How much of what passes for rationality really is rational, and how much is rationalization?

RATIONALITY AND THE EGO

The rationality of behavior is approached via the concept of the ego, defined as that part of the personality which deals with reality. The concept "ego" is best thought of as a locus of functions, not a thing. The strong ego is the one that handles reality well; the weak one handles reality poorly.

DEFENSIVE AND AUTONOMOUS FUNCTIONS

Ego structure is the total personality. It enables us to grasp all aspects of the individual's functioning. The ego involves both *defensive* and *autonomous functions.* These are separated for theoretical purposes; in practice they exist side by side. Knowledge of the autonomous ego postdates Freud, who paid relatively little attention to this side of the problem.

DEFENSES

Different personalities use different defenses. This opens the way to a new diagnostic classification in terms of defensive patterns, rather than in terms of overt symptomatology, a change of inestimable value in seeing people in more dynamic terms.

EGO STRENGTH AND MENTAL ILLNESS

With the ego concept a new definition of neurosis and psychosis becomes possible: personality disorder is to be viewed in the light of ego strength or ego weakness. Since these interact heavily with developmental stages, maturity and regression again play significant roles. Yet there is a great difference, in that the various ego functions can be specified in detail, so that regression need not be looked at in such global terms.

EGO DEVELOPMENT

Like everything else in the personality, the ego develops from birth to maturity. This development can be traced in a general way here; a more detailed discussion is given in various places.

1. At birth the infant has virtually no ego. Hartmann refers to this as the *undifferentiated state,* from which id and ego develop separately.

2. Ego development depends (a) on the interpersonal climate (give the child love and it will grow) and (b) on stimulation.

(a) *Interpersonal climate.* Love is the atmosphere in which a strong ego grows. Like growth in any other biological realm, all that is necessary is to provide the atmosphere that is most conducive to it; the growth will then take care of itself.

(b) *Stimulation.* This statement has to be modified to allow for the effects of stimulation. Freud generally took the position that overstimulation was harmful; the nervous system is a system that is designed to get rid of stimuli. Today there is a tendency to take the opposite point of view: sensory deprivation is as bad as, if not worse than, overstimulation. Clearly a proper balance is necessary to maximal ego development.

In practice the actual ego results from the combination of strengths and weaknesses in the family, together with the kinds and degrees of stimulation encountered. (In this connection the effect of a stimulating person, other than the parents, on the child must be considered. This is especially relevant to the analytic procedure.)

3. Defenses are an inevitable part of the growth process, especially before puberty. The child is not yet strong enough (ego too weak) to cope with the anxieties that face it. Hence it builds up defenses. Personality is thus a combination of anxiety plus defenses. Once the growth process is completed, anxieties can be handled in a mature way, and so theoretically no defenses are required.

4. Before the superego is developed, we should rather speak of the precursors of defenses, since they are not yet deeply internalized. The child before five is still highly malleable. It should be investigated whether the persistence of the personality patterns is due to the stability of the environment or their internalization or routinization. From this point of view, latency is the period when the defenses become fully stabilized.

5. Defenses owe their strength to their association with the id. This is an extension of the old principle that the symptom is a combination of sexual gratification and the defense against it. This is why occasionally a defense breaks down and the id crashes through, and also why there is a continuum from the sick to the healthy. Defenses are nourished by the id; those that are unconnected with it wither away and die.

6. The less defensiveness, the more ego, and vice versa. The ideal in the adult is a defenseless personality.

7. The constitutional factor in the ego is still unknown. There must be some, since differences are visible among neonates virtually from the time that they are born.

8. The development of the autonomous ego goes hand in hand with that of the defensive; the two are separated for theoretical reasons. Their intricate interrelationships can be systematically explored.

9. The defense mechanisms are much broader than those ordinarily listed in the textbooks. For example, the id may be a defense against the ego or the ego against the id. What therapy attemps to do is to trace the precise psychic sequence from the anxiety on. Sometimes this will involve a reaction formation or a regression; more often it will be

expressed more readily in ordinary human terms. For example, attachment to an unsuitable object is a defense against the loss of the mother, or against the idea that nobody will ever want him (or her) again.

HISTORICAL NOTE

Other schools can be understood in terms of overemphasis on either the ego or the id. Adler, Sullivan, and Horney tend to overemphasize the ego, and say little or nothing about the id. Jung overemphasizes the id (he stresses that we are creatures in the hands of instinct, which are deeply unconscious forces over which man has little control). Thus the Freudian system remains the most balanced.

At the same time it must be remembered that the Freudian system is still in the process of evolving, not a finished product. Many Freudians who place extreme emphasis on ego psychology generally underestimate the role that parents play in personality formation. Many other points of difference could be cited. Each topic must be considered on its own merits.

THE DEFENSIVE EGO: THE MAJOR DEFENSES

Freud and his co-workers described a number of defense mechanisms used to ward off anxiety. Although the concept has been broadened, little of an essential nature has been changed since. Detailed investigation of the defense mechanisms should explore (a) their dynamic, genetic, and economic functioning; (b) their roots in parent-child interaction; and (c) their maintenance (or discontinuance) in relation to the social system (other people).

1. *Repression* remains the basic defense, entering into all others. The essence of repression lies in pushing back into the unconscious that which produces anxiety. However, it is rare that repression is completely successful, so that two important consequences occur: (a) the repressed material comes out in a variety of derivative ways; (b) at times it breaks through directly, producing the phenomenon of the return of the repressed.

2. *Regression* is the reemergence of modes of mental functioning that were characteristic of the psychic activity of the individual during earlier periods of development.

3. *Reaction formation* is a type of repression in which the counter-cathexis is manifest and which therefore succeeds in avoiding oft-repeated acts of secondary repression; this avoidance is brought about by making a once-and-for-all definitive change of the personality.

The triad of defenses of repression, reaction formation, and regression is sometimes known as the neurotic triad, in contrast to denial, projection, and isolation, which form a psychotic triad.

4. *Denial* relates to external reality, whereas the other defenses relate to the instincts. Since it involves a disavowal of part of reality, it is the forerunner, if not the manifestation, of a psychosis.

5. *Depersonalization* is a form of denial; what is denied is the identity of the person, rather than the outside world.

6. *Projection* is the denial and projection of an impulse to some external person or object. It is the basic defense mechanism in paranoia. Because it places the impulse at such a distance, it makes treatment virtually impossible.

7. *Identification, introjection, incorporation* are all aspects of the process whereby another person is internalized and made part of oneself.

8. *Acting-out* can best be defined as an action, usually repetitive and compulsive, often self-destructive or self-damaging, which serves the unconscious purpose of resolving a repressed internal conflict by external means.

9. *Sublimation* is a socially approved expression of an instinctual impulse. Since "social approval" has become increasingly questionable as a criterion of mental health, the concept has lost much of its value, and is rarely seen in the contemporary literature.

10. *Neutralization* is defined by Hartmann as the change of both libidinal and aggressive energy away from the instinctual and toward a noninstinctual mode. It is urged by Hartmann as the "normal" solution; this, however, is questionable.

11. *Isolation* separates out the painful aspects of any experience from the unpainful and deprives them of their cathexis.

12. *Displacement.* Here an event, memory, or feeling that is painful is shifted to some other sphere where it can be experienced as less painful.

DEFENSE AND THE CHILDHOOD BACKGROUND

A defense mechanism is genetically a way of warding off parental anger. Consequently the classification and understanding of defense mechanisms must be tied in with the understanding of the early familial environment.

Repression

From this point of view, the simplest defense of all is *repression*, which arises in the following way: An impulse is forbidden by the parents, whenever it is expressed by the child. However, the parents are satisfied with the disappearance of the impulse and demand nothing further from the child. In order to satisfy this kind of parental demand, the child at first merely has to keep the wish in his mind. This creates a good deal of tension, so he then takes the next step, which is to put the thought out of mind. As a result, the usual inhibited, repressed kind of individual so common in our culture is developed (WASP personality structure).

Regression

In this defense, the parents demand not merely a blocking off of the wish, but an infantilization of the personality, in greater or lesser degree. In many cases, this infantilization seems to occur contrary to the will of the parents; a typical case is that of regression to soiling or incontinence upon the birth of a new baby. These incidents tend to pass if the parents do not receive any gratification from the infantile fears of the child. Ordinarily, the infantilization plays into the wishes of the parent, in some unconscious manner. Perhaps this is one reason why parents are so reluctant to do anything about their children's regressions. The expression "He'll outgrow it" helps to keep the child at the infantile level which the parent relishes.

Reaction Formation

Reaction formation occurs when the parent demands not only a repression, but a continual affirmation of the opposite. It is most often seen in cases of a reaction formation against anger. The child who develops such a reaction formation must not only avoid any manifestations of anger, but must provide continual proofs of love to the parents, in order to show that he really has no anger. In later life, he likewise has to provide continual displays of love to other people, again to avoid any imputation that he might be angry in any way.

Denial

Denial is a more global reaction than repression, and it is used primarily in terms of a denial of reality, whereas repression is used in terms of the repression of an impulse. In denial there is an identification with the parents, who exercise a similar denial. Because the parents have reached a stage where the denial does not necessarily interfere with their functioning, this goes unnoticed. In the child, it is cause for attention only because he has not yet navigated some of the major developmental stages.

Projection

In projection, there is insistence that an impulse belongs to someone else, rather than to oneself. This kind of insistence comes from a childhood environment in which one parent wanted the child to take sides against the other. More usually, it is the mother-son or mother-daughter against the father. Less common but quite frequent is the combination of father and daughter against the mother. In the childhood background of these people, what is striking is the parental insistence that they not only deny the impulses involved, but actively assert that it is the other parent who is at fault. Typically then and not surprisingly, one or both of the parents are found to be quite paranoid. Again, this paranoia goes unnoticed because the parent is an adult, who has the right to manage his own affairs, and is not a patient.

Isolation

In isolation a gap widens between the sexual and the aggressive impulses. Usually the aggressive impulses are stronger, strong enough to take over the personality almost entirely. Denial and projection are frequently found in combination with isolation. The childhood background of these people is one in which there was an extraordinary taboo imposed on sexuality. Any mention of it was bound to arouse the deepest suspicions of the parents, and bring on the child the severest punishment. Many times the child is able to stand up to such a total isolation because there are other, favorable forces in the environment or because there are impulses so strong that they cannot be put out of mind. At other times, the isolation becomes complete and the pathology in the personality becomes more and more acute.

Acting-Out

Acting-out should more properly be called destructive action. In this kind of action, the childhood background is one in which the parents are able to hold back their own propensities for certain types of actions, but incite the child to carry them out. The parents derive gratification from the child's acting-out. Even when the acting-out seems to be a total rebellion against the parent, as is so often the case in the adolescent, it is often clear that the parent would like to behave in this way if only he had the opportunity.

Identification

In identification, the parent insists that the child should behave in exactly the same way he does. The emphasis is on obedience, which is made most explicit by copying the parental behavior in all its details. In the defense of identification with the aggressor the child identifies with the aggressive components of the parental behavior. Similar forms of identification, however, are found with all aspects of the parental behavior.

The Double Bind

In the double bind, first described by Bateson, the child is exposed on the one hand to a command, and on the other hand to a punishment if he obeys the command. This double bind is characteristic of the development of the schizophrenic child. What it means in relation to the parents is that the parents can never really be satisfied. Since the child cannot satisfy the parent, he then resorts to the device of leaving the field. Since the parents will not leave him alone, this device of leaving the field also serves the purpose of getting away from the pressures that they put upon him.

EGO STRENGTH AND EGO WEAKNESS

There are many more defense mechanisms than those listed. What has to be described in each case is the way in which the child evades the anxiety created by parental anger, by a variety of mechanisms.

The concepts of *ego weakness and ego strength* can supplant the older concepts of diagnostic categories. An ego is strong when it can confront the superego. It is weak to the extent that it fails in each of these functions. The normal ego is one that can handle all these demands. To the extent that the ego breaks down in any of these requirements, the individual becomes sick, engaging in repetitive stereotyped self-destructive and maladaptive behavior.

It is often found that the ego is weak in one area and strong in another. This observation confounds those who wish to rely on some oversimplified diagnosis such as schizophrenia or latent schizophrenia. It is necessary to specify the particular areas in which the ego functions properly and the areas in which it does not. The work of Bellak and his associates on ego functions and schizophrenia (1973) is a pioneering attempt to work out the details of this concept.

Defensiveness keeps the ego weak. What was useful to placate the parents in childhood becomes a burden in dealing with adults in real life. Hence the ideally healthy person is one without defenses.

THE AUTONOMOUS EGO

EGO AUTONOMY: PRIMARY AND SECONDARY

The "autonomy" of the ego refers to its autonomy from the id. By *primary ego autonomy* is meant those ego functions that are inherently independent of the id. By *secondary autonomy* is meant those functions that were at one time determined by id drives, but have now lost contact with them. Both forms of autonomy play a significant role in human experience.

Under primary ego autonomy are included the cognitive functions, memory, thinking, perception, and learning. In each of these it is possible to separate an active or unstimulated kind of process from a passive or stimulated kind of process. Evidence for the significance of this spontaneous activity is overwhelming; to begin with, it is seen in the material on dreams. Psychoanalysis has dealt primarily with the active, unstimulated processes (internal), while academic psychology has dealt with the passive, stimulated processes (external). Obviously a coalescence of the two approaches would be most fruitful.

It may be noted that in more recent years academic psychology has shifted its main focus increasingly to cognitive processes. The older dream that general laws of learning would be discovered from which all of psychological functioning could then be inferred, which Hull (1943) made explicit, has come up against so many disappointments that it is gradually disappearing. Hence the shift to cognition, since human beings obviously deal with cognitions, which have to be understood in their own terms.

Historically Freud never made his position entirely clear on this point. At times he wrote as if instincts were the only motivating forces in human beings, while at other times he explicitly recognized the "ego-instincts" or what would be called today the autonomous cognitive factors. Yet in his structural formulation, in 1923, everything was in theory originally derived from the id, in that the ego was an offshoot of the id, while the superego is an offshoot of the ego; hence in that formulation, strictly speaking, there is no room for an autonomous ego, except for the defenses that acquire secondary autonomy. Other analysts remained equally confused in this area.

It remained for Heinz Hartmann, in his book *Ego Psychology and the Problem of Adaptation* (1939), to set forth the necessary theoretical assumptions that would allow psychoanalysis to embrace all of psychology in a meaningful way.

Hartmann's main point is that the early analytic emphasis on the exclusive importance of the drives was an error. There is an inborn mental apparatus that develops regardless of the id. This is what we call the autonomous ego. Naturally it is related to the id, but it is not its direct descendant. In any function, somatic or psychic, it is possible to distinguish the contributions of the autonomous ego and of the defensive ego. Theoretically the approach is to discover the autonomous development of the various ego functions, to uncover the psychosexual development with its ego defense mechanisms, and then to combine these two branches of knowledge to explain any particular phenomenon.

In general, the discovery of the autonomous development of the various ego functions is the province of nonanalytic psychology and physiology. The older psychoanalytic explanations (thinking equals hallucinatory wish fulfillment, amnesia equals repression, etc.) fall by the board here; they are incorrect.

On the other hand, what the academic psychologist discovers is an artifact of his approach. Human beings behave that way only under certain circumstances (Klein: limiting circumstances). Hence to understand the functioning human being a combination of the two avenues is needed.

It is not possible within the confines of this book to offer a complete theory of any of the cognitive functions, even if that were feasible at the present time. What will be concentrated on here is the emotional interferences with cognitions, or more technically, the id interferences with "normal" ego functioning.

It is often difficult to spell out what this normal ego functioning is. G. S. Klein (1959) has suggested that the laws of perception developed in the academic experimental laboratories are specific only to a particular state of consciousness, and that the functional importance of these laws must be understood in terms of the structure and dominant orientations of that particular state. It is the state of consciousness characterizing behavior when one's conscious intentions are to master, to communicate, and to evaluate the properties of things—a state mobilized to an extreme in the laboratory perceptual task. In psychophysical studies there is brought to bear on response a state of consciousness that guarantees an effective appraisal of reality, sharp distinctions between wish and reality, the certain and the uncertain. It is for this state and about this state that perceptual theories have described their laws. Very possibly, Klein argues, most of the laws thus far formulated for perception have restricted validity for this state alone.

MEMORY

Memory has been studied intensively for more than a hundred years by a variety of methods.

Even without further investigation, memory is seen to be variable. Some people have a fantastic capacity to remember numbers, others names or faces. Even phenomenal memory in one area can be accompanied by poor achievements in others. However, *idiots savants* are no longer found, now that modern intelligence tests exist. When a person has a remarkable score in one area and complete incapacity in all others, the expert nowadays would ascribe it to emotional factors rather than a peculiarity of his brain.

Active (Unstimulated) vs. Passive (Stimulated) Memories

As in all the cognitive functions, active memories can be distinguished from passive, stimulated from unstimulated. The passive ones (stimulated) stay closer to the classical laws; the active ones (unstimulated) stay closer to psychodynamic explanations. The origins of these two kinds of memories are different.

Psychodynamic Memories

The psychoanalytic memories are always long-term, or have some reference to a long-term structure inside the mind. By contrast academic psychology has experimented largely with short-term memories. The few studies that relate to LTM (long-term memories) have tended to confirm the supposition of an emotionally organized matrix of memories which influences present-day mental functioning; e.g., Bartlett's famous study of the retention of stories (1932), or Allport's study of the spread of rumors during World War II (Allport and Postman, 1947).

Associations to psychodynamic memories always lead back to something deeply meaningful to the individual, even if the immediate material is seemingly indifferent or trivial in nature (see the relevant discussion in connection with dreams, where it is shown that any seemingly indifferent or trivial material was really directly related to the core concerns of the person). For this reason the forgetting of recent memories (e.g., the forgetting of dreams) would therefore be emotionally determined because of its connections with the deeper structures of the mind.

Psychodynamic memories are organized in terms of (1) meaning, (2) concomitant fantasies, and (3) ego structure. By contrast, non-dynamic memories may either be unorganized or superficially organized. Since they are not related to the deeper concerns of the individual, they are not retained with the same force.

The storage-retrieval model is one that fits the data of psychoanalysis well. Stored memories are maintained in reasonably organized form. It would seem that many of the memories that psychoanalysis deals with are stored in the form of generalizations (e.g., women are dangerous like mother; this woman is therefore dangerous).

Active retrieval goes on all the time. The mind is always active; it either perceives or fantasizes; quiescence is relative rather than absolute. All this accounts well for the properties of free associations; e.g., Freud says that he adopted the method because there will always be some association, in contrast to hypnosis, which fails to work much of the time.

PERCEPTION

Although perception is just about the oldest topic in psychology, it is only fairly recently that the relationship between perception and personality has come to be appreciated. Unlike memory, which plays a central role in the psychoanalytic treatment process, perception seems peripheral to the whole affair. Unless it breaks down entirely as in schizophrenia, the analyst is apt to ignore it. It was only as knowledge of ego psychology accumulated, and as the patient population was extended more and more to the normal population, that the interaction between personality and perception came to be appreciated.

Degree of Autonomy of Perception

However, it still remains true that the percept is, all things considered, the most autonomous aspect of ego functioning. Even deteriorated schizophrenics may be able to maintain much of their perceptual apparatus intact. This explains why the academic-cognitive approach has concentrated so heavily on perception: it is least interfered with by emotional factors.

Perception and Personality: Witkin's Classic Study

Nevertheless, in ambiguous situations there is a close link between perception and personality. The classic work that established this point for psychologists was that by Witkin and his colleagues, *Personality Through Perception* (1954). They showed that when the perceptual field is unclear, people tend to orient themselves either in a field-dependent or a field-independent way, and that these cognitive variables are closely related to dimensions of personality. Later other investigators demonstrated the existence of a variety of *cognitive controls* (Klein et al., 1959; Dember, 1960). Among the important methods of control are *perceptual defense* and *perceptual bias*. In extreme situations motivational effects on perception are manifest; in many ordinary everyday situations motivation plays a minor role. The determination of when motivation is important and when not is an empirical question.

THINKING

Because of the basic role of the fundamental rule of free association in the psychoanalytic process, thinking has always had a central part in psychoanalytic theory. Some topics, such as free association itself, and the fantasy life of man, have been explored far more fully by psychodynamically oriented theoreticians than any other. Others, which play a relatively small part in the therapeutic process, such as problem solving, have tended to be ignored.

Active (Unstimulated) vs. Passive (Stimulated) Thought

As with the other cognitive functions, a distinction must be drawn between active and passive, unstimulated and stimulated. Active, unstimulated thinking includes associations, imagery, dreams, daydreams, language formation, symbolism, and concept formation. Passive, stimulated thinking is largely confined to problem solving. Again, since the experimental method lends itself particularly well to stimulated processes, the academic work has centered very heavily on problem solving.

Free Association

Free association was specifically adopted in order to get at the underlying unconscious material. The perceptual apparatus is reduced to a minimum, which allows the fantasies to come to the fore. Free association includes a mixture of memories, fantasies, bodily experiences, and associations of all kinds.

Actually, free association lends itself rather readily to experimental manipulation, and that it has not been used in that way can only be attributed to the rejection of dynamic theory, without which the productions would not make much sense. In the clinical use of the projective techniques, however, free association is often adopted, as a supplement to the actual responses.

Bellak (1961) feels that associating as a process is best understood as predicated upon the oscillating function of the ego, involving first letting controls go, and then restoring them. The emphasis is on the relative reduction of cognitive ego functions. Relative ego participation in the first phase (letting controls go) is more pronounced in associating than in the dream, hypnagogic elements, and preconscious fantasy, but less so than in some daydreams, responses to projective tests, and purposive planning.

DAYDREAMING

In daydreaming, as the word implies, the person dreams while awake. Hence the principles that apply to dream interpretation must apply here, at least to some extent. The difference is that there is more ego control present in the daydream. This usually results in less distortion, and more open expressions of wish fulfillment. Studies of daydreams and daydreamers by Varendonck (1921) and Singer (1966) lead to no new theoretical conclusions. As with Freudian slips, the unconscious breaks through in various ways, depending on the ego structure of the daydreamer.

Fantasy and the Ego

The many problems encountered can be resolved by the concept of the secondary autonomy of the ego. Some scientists say that science is pursued because initially it gratified some id drives. But then it acquires autonomy to such an extent that the person can function there at a high level because the id meaning of what he is doing has been completely repressed into the unconscious. When the repressed material returns, the person has a breakdown, from which he usually manages to recover (Fine, 1966).

Within the framework of ego psychology, then, to understand a fantasy requires a thorough exploration of the total ego structure. Id, ego, and superego, as well as native endowment and external circumstances, may and usually do play roles in the end product. A fantasy can be defined as any product of the mind other than a perception of the real world; thus it would include memories, associations, dreams, daydreams, and artistic productions. The decisive question is whether the fantasy serves a constructive or destructive function in the person's life. Usually the answer will not be a simple one. Rather it will often be found that in some respects the fantasy life is constructive, in others destructive.

Summary

Other aspects of the thinking process such as language and creativity will be treated in other chapters. The material presented here shows that there is an intimate connection in all thinking activities between the ego and the id. The differentiation between the autonomous and the defensive ego is made on purely theoretical grounds; both will always play a role, though in varying degrees. Poor intellectual functioning, i.e., poor in relation to some calculated theoretical capacity for any individual, is more a sign of emotional interference than of anything else. This would explain why one of the common findings in any kind of psychotherapy is some improvement, sometimes dramatic, in one or more areas of intellectual functioning.

LEARNING

Learning theory, as it has been developed by experimental and behavioral psychologists, seems to offer a perfect paradigm for the autonomous ego. Indeed, perhaps the most prominent, or at least vociferous, proponent of learning theory on the present-day scene, B. F. Skinner, regards such concepts as emotion, hope, wishes, and the like as pure anthropomorphism, and wishes to do away with them, relying only on objectively determined "schedules of reinforcement." Yet, as has been noted, as time has gone on, psychologists have become less and less convinced of the ubiquitous significance of learning theory, and have turned increasingly to cognition and other aspects of the human being.

The wide range of theories within "learning theory" proper is sufficient to show that the data are not at all clear-cut, even in easily replicable animal experimentation. When these are extended to human beings, the disagreements become even wider and more fundamental.

CHARACTER STRUCTURE

The conception of character cannot be said to be well crystallized. There are different ideas stemming from different periods of the development of the science. Even today these ideas are rather poorly coordinated, e.g., the relationship between the individual and the social.

BASIC IDEAS

Certain ideas are basic: (1) character involves the elaboration of anxieties and the defenses against them; (2) character involves repetitive patterns of behavior; (3) character is related to the social milieu; in fact, every social milieu rewards certain types of personalities and disapproves of others (this creates statistical normality, not analytic normality); (4) character embraces the total life functioning of the individual, i.e., the autonomic as well as the defensive functions.

CLASSIFICATION OF CHARACTER

The more systematic analytic description of character types is still in a highly unsatisfactory state. Various classifications have been suggested, but none has caught on. Fenichel (1945, p. 467) defines character as the habitual mode of bringing into harmony the tasks presented by internal demands and by the external world, which is necessarily a function of the constant, organized, and integrating part of the personality which is the ego. The question of character would thus be the question of when and how the ego acquires the qualities by which it habitually adjusts itself to the demands of instinctual drives and of the external world, and later also of the superego (not enough stress is placed on parent-child interaction). Also to be considered here is Waelder's (1960) principle of multiple function, i.e., the tendency of the organism to get the maximum done with the minimum of effort. Thus those character traits are favored which gratify the greatest number of demands.

CHARACTER "ARMOR"

In the understanding of character a significant advance after Freud was made by Wilhelm Reich in his book *Character Analysis* (only the first part, 1933). Reich sees character as a chronic alteration of the ego which one might describe as a rigidity. Its meaning is the protection of the ego against external and internal dangers. It can be called an armor. The armoring of the ego takes place as a result of fear of punishment, at the expense of id energies, and contains the prohibitions of early education.

Reich contrasts the genital character with the neurotic character. This contrast is not a rigid one. It is based on a quantitative criterion, the extent of either direct sexual gratification or libido stasis, and so there are all kinds of transitions between the two ideal types. Reich's characterology was based on instinctual development, frustration, and armoring.

CHARACTER STRUCTURE AND THE CULTURE

A further step was taken by Kardiner, who in *The Psychological Frontiers of Society* (1945) offered the first comprehensive integration of psychodynamic and anthropological data. Every culture has a basic personality type that is characteristic of it; others must be seen as deviations from that type. The institutions of the culture are designed to perpetuate that type. Kardiner feels that Freud's signal and durable achievement was an appraisal of man from the point of view of biography (one should remember that Freud was his analyst for only four months). He described a number of key integrational systems: maternal care, induction of affectivity, early disciplines, sexual disciplines, institutionalized sibling attitudes, induction into work, puberty, marriage, character of participation in society, factors that keep the society together, projective systems (religion, folklore), reality systems derived from empirical or projective sources, arts and crafts techniques, and techniques of production.

It is clear that this schema provides the basis for a thorough analysis of the personality. It is equally clear that such an analysis does not lend itself to any short-cut descriptions, such as "anal" or "oral" societies.

APPROACHES TO CHARACTER DESCRIPTION

To give a total description of any person's character structure would involve an enormous amount of information. Included in it would have to be descriptions of the id, the ego, the superego, anxieties, defenses, conscious and unconscious forces, interpersonal relations, significant features of the life history, major defense mechanisms employed, interests, attitudes, habits, characteristic patterns of handling the world, symptoms (if any), ideals, goals, ambitions, and many other features. Necessarily such a description would have to be made largely for theoretical purposes, since in the actual clinical situation it would be hopelessly impractical. Nor has it been possible to reach any generalizations on the basis of such exhaustive compilations of data.

What has been done rather is to isolate certain recurrent themes in the life situation and/or life history of the individual, to draw these themes into a consistent constellation, which may or may not be seen as the core of the person, and to try to tie up these recurrent themes with the rest of the individual's functioning. What that boils down to is actually that certain salient features of the personality are selected on the basis of general knowledge of psychodynamic theory, and their significance for the person's life demonstrated. Naturally that leaves to the "averages" many other aspects of the person's life. It tends to describe a core constellation rather than a total personality, primarily because the total personality is too complicated to describe. It is with these caveats that the characterological descriptions found in the literature should be approached.

CHAPTER 9

Language and Creativity

LANGUAGE AS A BASIC HUMAN NEED

In the twelfth-century chronicle of Salimbene a linguistic experiment of Frederick II is reported. King Frederick wanted to find out what kind of speech and what manner of speech children would have when they grew up, if they spoke to no one beforehand. So he bade foster mothers and nurses to suckle the children, to bathe and wash them, but in no way to prattle or speak with them, for he wanted to learn whether they would speak the Hebrew language, which is the oldest, or Greek or Latin or Arabic, or perhaps the language of their parents. But he labored in vain because all the children died. They could not live without petting and joyful faces and loving words.

The story illustrates beautifully the age-old awareness of the infant's need for vocal interchange with mother. Language, in Sapir's (1921) definition, is a purely human method of communicating ideas, emotions, and desires by means of a system of voluntarily produced symbols. These symbols are in the first instance auditory and they are produced by the so-called organs of speech. Language, Sapir emphasizes, is specifically human. Together with conceptual functioning it forms the rational endowment of mankind. But while it subserves rational thinking, its major function in human affairs is communication. It is in terms of the development of linguistic communication and its disturbances that the information about language can best be organized.

PSYCHOLINGUISTICS: THE EGO PSYCHOLOGY
OF LANGUAGE

In the past several decades linguistics, or psycholinguistics, has advanced to a stage where it can be referred to as a science. Such a designation is somewhat inaccurate. It is rather more appropriate to see linguistics as the ego psychology of language, which has established certain basic facts about human beings.

Among these are the following: Language exists in all cultures. Certain universals are found, such as the manipulation of basic sounds (phonemes) and meaningful units (morphemes), although the phonemes and morphemes will vary from one language to another. There are no truly simple languages; all show greater or lesser degrees of compexity. Very often languages developed by primitive cultures are more complex than those developed by more advanced ones. Linguistic skills develop at similar rates in all cultures, which supports Chomsky's contention that language is an expression of the *a priori*, or innate mental activity. Language is strongly influenced by culture, which has led to the growth of the field of sociolinguistics. However, the extreme Whorf-Sapir hypothesis that language determines the psychological climate in which each culture lives, and that this is different from one culture to another, must be rejected as too extreme.

COMMUNICATION

1. Schizophrenia, the last ditch of mental illness, is obviously a disorder of communication. Even to the layman the major characteristic of the schizophrenic is that he is "unintelligible." Actually he comes to the attention of his social circle or professionals only when his utterances and/or actions reach the point of unintelligibility, even though more careful examination would have revealed serious sources of difficulty much sooner. In principle the seemingly "crazy" utterances of the schizophrenic can be decoded and understood.

2. It was realized quite early that dreams are a form of communication, and the explication of the language of dreams marks a noticeable advance in psychology.

3. Many neurotic symptoms, such as hysterical conversions of all kinds, are symbolic ways of communicating with other people. The very first patient in psychoanalytic history, Anna O. (Freud and Breuer, 1895), who invented the term "the talking cure," had a lingustic problem, in that for a while she could speak only English instead of her native German.

4. The process of psychoanalysis focuses in the most intimate detail on the ways in which two people communicate with one another, both verbally and nonverbally. Actually, it could be said that interpretation in psychoanalysis represents the attempt to put into adult words what the patient is trying to communicate in other ways, either by actions or by linguistic utterances from an earlier stage of development.

5. There has been a strong and growing realization that the entire process of alienation, neurosis, and psychosis represents a failure in communication. As with all mental phenomena, there is a continuum of gradations from the normal to the psychotic, indicating that difficulties in communication are widespread.

6. The extraordinary power displayed by propaganda in the totalitarian countries has emphasized that communication varies widely from the meanings of the words used. George Orwell in his mordant novel *1984* satirized this as "newthink," which could prove beyond the shadow of a doubt that black is white.

MANIPULATIVE AND EXPRESSIVE COMMUNICATION

A primary distinction must be drawn between *manipulative* communication and *expressive,* similar to that in emotion. Expressive communication is a manifestation of the autonomous ego, and suits the communication to the rational purpose for which it is intended. Manipulative communication, however, as the name implies, is designed to manipulate another person to do something, either consciously or unconsciously. A certain amount of manipulative communication is quite consciously dishonest, even cynical, as in propaganda. But a good deal of it is unconsciously determined. The manipulation is then directed primarily at the introjected superego, secondarily at the other person. The success or failure of the manipulation depends on the similarity between the introject and the other person. In schizophrenia communication is generally manipulative, and generally fails because the outside person is so different from the patient's superego. In less disturbed conditions the outcome will naturally vary.

Rose Spiegel (1959) suggests a fivefold classification of (manipulative) communication: (1) grossly destructive, (2) authoritarian, (3) disjunctive, (4) pseudocommunication, and (5) noncommunication.

An important but neglected area of communication is the lie. Lying may be a symptom of a deeper disturbance, as in the pathological liar, or it may be a sign of a healthy ego, who is aware that the communication of the truth may be more painful than telling a "little white lie." Ludwig (1965) rightly comments that most of his material has had to be taken from literary rather than clinical sources. No doubt the psychoanalyst's moralistic aversion to lying, especially since he places such a premium on telling the absolute truth, contributes to the disinterest expressed in this subject.

JOKES: A UNIVERSAL FORM OF COMMUNICATION

Freud's book on jokes, still the classic treatment of the subject, sets forth clearly the thesis that the joke is a form of communication. He mentions (1905c, p. 143)

> . . . the generally recognized experience that no one can be content with having a joke for himself alone. . . . I myself cannot laugh at a *joke* that has occurred to me, that I have made, in spite of the unmistakable enjoyment that the joke gives me. It is possible that *my need to communicate the joke to someone else is in some way connected with the laughter produced by it,* which is denied to me but is manifest in the other person. [Italics mine.]

The pleasurable effect of jokes depends on two factors: a special *technique,* and the *tendency* of the joke. In a joke with a play on words the commonest technique is that of condensation. In a joke wth a thought behind it, several other technical means may be employed: displacement, establishment of unexpected connections, indirect presentation, psychic economy—all of these are known from dreams. As to the aim of jokes, the harmless ones merely offer an expenditure of pleasure; the tendentious ones, however, derive from the release of instinctual impulses that otherwise have to be inhibited is found in the sexual and aggressive wishes. In a subsequent paper, in 1927 ("On Humor"), written after the structural system had been formulated, Freud attributes some of the pleasure derived to the mitigation of the severity of the superego, thus again making the joke an exercise in communication.

Joking Relationships

A striking confirmation of Freud's thesis that the joke is a specialized form of social communication which serves to give some release to anthropological material on joking relationships. In a large number of societies joking relationships are institutionalized, i.e., they are permitted within certain relationships but tabooed in others.

Murdock (1949) has examined these joking relationships in 250 societies. In general he finds that the joking relationship tends to obtain between relatives standing in a potential sexual relationship to each other. The wife stands in a special nontabooed relationship. The fact that neither avoidance nor joking nor license is associated with the spouse in any of the sample societies reflects the economic cooperation, sexual cohabitation, and partnership in child-rearing that are universally characteristic of this relationship.

SYMBOLISM

In the popular mind psychoanalysis is identified with the free interpretation of symbols. Of course this is quite erroneous. It is true, however, that the elucidation of the symbolic process, undertaken originally by Freud and his followers, is one of the most important procedures available in understanding human communication.

THE CLASSICAL (JONES-FERENCZI) THEORY OF SYMBOLISM

The best account of the classical theory of symbolism, which has also been referred to as the Jones-Ferenczi theory, is in Jones's paper "The Theory of Symbolism" (1916). The discussion can follow his account.

Symbolism is a form of indirect representation which is adopted because direct representation would arouse too much anxiety. All symbolism betokens a relative incapacity for either apprehension or presentation, primarily the former; this may be either affective or intellectual in origin, the first of these two factors being the more important. As a result of this relative incapacity the mind reverts to a simpler type of mental process, and the greater the incapacity, the more primitive is the type of mental process reverted to. Hence in the most usual forms the symbol is the kind of mental process that costs least effort—it is sensorial, usually visual; visual because in retrospect most perceptual memories become converted into visual forms, this in turn being partly due to the ease of visual representation.

CONCRETENESS

For the same reason symbolism is always concrete, since concrete mental processes are both easier and more primitive than any other.

Most forms of symbolism therefore may be described as the automatic substituting of a concrete idea, characteristically in the form of its sensory image, for another idea that is more or less difficult of access, and which may be hidden or unconscious, and which has one or more attributes in common with the symbolizing idea.

FEELING

The essential difficulty that goes with all forms of symbolism is in the adequate apprehending (and therefore also in the conveying) of feeling. This is doubtless to be ascribed to the innumerable inhibitions of feeling which are operative throughout the mind, and which exhibit a more concentrated force in some regions than in others. It is therefore to be expected that the most typical and highly developed forms of symbolism will be found in connection with those regions.

UNCONSCIOUS ROOTS

In this strict sense the two major characteristics of symbolism are (1) that the process is completely unconscious and (2) that the affect attached to the symbolized idea has not, insofar as the symbolism is concerned, been proved capable of sublimation. In both these respects symbolism differs from all other forms of indirect representation.

The typical attributes of true symbolism are: (1) representation of unconscious material; (2) constant meaning, or very limited scope for variation in meaning; (3) nondependence on individual factors only; (4) evolutionary basis; (5) linguistic connections between the symbol and the idea symbolized; (6) phylogenetic parallels with the symbolism as found in different cultures existing in myths, cults, religions, and so on.

UNIVERSAL FEATURES OF MYTHOLOGY

The study of myth has likewise revealed the universal need to make some sense out of the universe, to express that sense in dramatic form, and to pass that dramatic form on from one generation to the next. Kluckhohn (1960) has a good summary of the available research.

There are certain features of mythology that are apparently universal or have such wide distribution in space and time that their generality may be presumed to result from recurrent reactions of the human psyche to situations and stimuli of the same general order.

It has long been recognized that parallels among various cultural groups are widespread. In considering such parallels, some elementary cautions must be observed. First, levels of abstraction must be kept distinct. Second, mere comparison on the basis of the presence or absence of a trait are tricky and may well be misleading. Nevertheless, most of the comparisons must be made on the basis of presence or absence, since quantitative precision is not available.

Most anthropologists today would agree that throughout the world myths resemble one another to an extraordinary degree.

THE CREATION MYTH

Kluckhohn presents certain mythological themes that are virtually universal. One is the creation myth. This may seem too broad a category, yet Rooth (1957), on analyzing three hundred creation myths of the North American Indians, finds that most of them fit comfortably into eight types, and that seven of these types appear likewise in Eurasia.

WITCHCRAFT

There are two ways of reasoning that bulk prominently in all mythological systems. These are what Frazer called the "laws" of sympathetic magic (like causes like) and holophrastic magic (the part stands for the whole). These principles are particularly employed in one content area where the record is so full and exceptionless that one is justified in speaking of genuine cultural universals: witchcraft. The following themes seem to appear always and everywhere:

1. Were-animals who move about at night with miraculous speed, gathering in witches' sabbaths to work evil magic.

2. The notion that illness, emaciation, and eventual death can result from introducing by magical means some sort of noxious substance into the body of the victim.

3. A connection between incest and witchcraft.

The only cultural variations here concern minutiae: details of the magical techniques, which animals are portrayed, what kinds of witchcraft poisons are employed. (Analytically this would be interpreted as the bad mother projection.) The persistence of these beliefs cannot be understood except on the hypothesis that these images have a special congeniality for the human mind as a consequence of the relations of children to their parents and other childhood experiences that are universal rather than culture-bound.

This suggests that the interaction of a certain kind of biological apparatus in a certain kind of physical world with some inevitables of the human condition (the helplessness of infants, two parents of different sex, etc.) bring about some regularities in the formation of imaginative productions and powerful images.

Symbolism can thus be regarded as a universal activity of the human mind, and general principles derived originally from the interpretation of dreams are applicable everywhere.

CREATIVITY

To be mentally healthy involves a certain amount of creativity. This is one of the major surprising findings of modern psychology. "Creativity" is used here, however, in the sense of an attitude toward the world, a willingness to take a fresh look, to see things never seen before, to appreciate what has previously been ignored or denigrated.

ARTISTIC AND AESTHETIC ATTITUDES

A distinction can be drawn between the artistic and the aesthetic attitudes to life. In the artistic, there is a wish to create new forms, enjoy new experiences, seek out new ways of doing things, not just for the sake of novelty, but because doing so adds zest and meaning to life. It is a pleasure gain, in the sense of the term used in Chapter 3. The aesthete, on the other hand, wishes to appreciate what is there, to be a happy spectator, more content to look at the masterpieces that others have created than to try his own hand at some small undertaking that will leave others unmoved.

Both attitudes can be creative in life. The danger is that the artistic will deteriorate into a search for anything that is different, as in the drug addict, or in a sadistic murderer like Nero, while the aesthetic will bog down in a constant depreciation of the living by ceaselessly comparing them with the dead.

PSYCHOANALYSIS AND CREATIVITY

Psychoanalysis has had an intimate encounter with the creative in four ways. First, of course, by the analysis of creative personalities, i.e., those considered creative in the ordinary sense of the word—artists, writers, and scientists whose creative genius has placed an indelible stamp on modern civilization. Second, through the discovery, a result of serendipity really, that the average person possesses within himself unmeasured stores of ability which can be released through the process of psychoanalysis. The main characteristics of neurosis are stereotypy and repetition, and both of these militate against artistic achievement or aesthetic appreciation. Both derive from the constant struggle to overcome the anxieties encrusted within the personality from earliest childhood. It is not to be expected that a Shakespeare or a Picasso will be produced by analytic work; a certain degree of native genius is indispensable for that. But overcoming neurotic inhibitions may lead to all kinds of creative outlets hitherto undreamed of in the person's life. Third, by the study of innumerable famous artistic personalities, originally known as pathography (pathological biography), and now rebaptized psychohistory, psychoanalysts have been able to demonstrate the intimate connections between what a man produces and his inner conflicts. And finally through the technical device of the projective techniques, which are essentially artistic productions used in the service of understanding the personality, it has been possible to show that all persons can express their inner conflicts and desires in artistic media when asked and encouraged to do so.

THE CREATIVE ARTIST

A beginning can be made with the creative artist, who has been studied in most intimate detail. To begin with, he is closer to his id than the average person. He is in contact with wishes, desires, and instinctual impulses that are ordinarily repressed. Berkman (1972) in his biography of the painter Whistler uses the telling phrase "to seize the passing dream." The artist is indeed capable of seizing this passing dream, and the analogy is an apt one, for there too the dreamer must make use of primary process material, which has to be apprehended in a moment. Schneider (1950) calls this the creative thrust, which is then molded by the ego in an act of creative mastery. For true art both are necessary, id and ego, thrust and mastery, to seize the passing dream and to expand it. For the moment, however, our concern is only with the first of these, the id.

The artist, always attuned to a new inspiration, and thus closer to his id, becomes narcissistic. Inherently it is a form of healthy narcissism. The narcissism is transferred to his work, however, rather than remaining focused on himself. He shares his narcissistic experiences with an audience.

A number of possibilities now arise.

1. Frequently this process fails because the artist is dealing with dangerous material. The impulses come out too strongly, and he becomes more interested in gratifying them than in doing his work (cf. Gauguin). The gratification of the impulses without a brake carries with it all the dangers of psychosis, suicide, and self-destructive ac-

tivity which it does in persons who are not artists. This is one reason why pathology is so frequent among artists—they are playing too close to the fire (cf. Van Gogh).

2. When the process succeeds it may often do so by a regression in the service of the ego (Kris, 1952). Here the regression is permitted because the ego can make use of it. This is also done in analysis. Here too, however, the regression may become too far-reaching, and the artist may not come back so readily, or may not come back at all; the possibility of a malignant use of the regression is a factor that limits the applicability of classical psychoanalysis.

3. In another kind of artist there is an acceptance of impulse all the way around. This is the image of the Renaissance man—a hearty individual capable of enjoying life to the full. Rank (1932) saw this kind of man as the normal, in contrast to the conforming average and the will-crippled neurotic. (This fact can be used therapeutically: a patient with an oversupply of libido can be encouraged to move into artistic expression.)

4. Quite often the artist remains stuck in his narcissism. He has intimate contact with a small portion of reality, but outside of that sphere he is no different from the ordinary inhibited man.

5. Then again the narcissism may become so severe that it takes the place of the art. In that event the artist no longer has the buffer of his artistic production—he becomes directly interested in displaying himself. Such an increase in narcissism frequently leads to a greater or lesser degree of psychosis.

6. Because of the opportunity for narcissistic gratification, many people are attracted to art as an avenue of release for their narcissism. They may have little or no talent for art, or little or no interest in it. They play artist in order to be bohemian, not bohemian because it is indispensable for their art.

7. The narcissistic release may be temporarily frightening, so that artistic productivity comes to a halt—the creative block. This is undoubtedly the most frequent reason why artists come to analysis. It is readily understood from the analysis of the circumstances.

8. The narcissistic absorption may become so fatiguing that the artist gives up his art in order to return to ordinary living. This is not so much creative block as creative fatigue. Sometimes the retreat is permanent; more often it is temporary.

ART AS A SOCIAL PROCESS

Besides being a release of impulse, art is also a social process—it is intimately related in the artist's mind to what other people are thinking or saying. The artist's self-image plays an important role here—particularly in modern times his self-image as one who comes closer to ultimate truth than any other man. In this image he often sees himself challenged by the psychoanalyst; hence his antipathy to the analyst.

Once the relevance of art as a social process is established, ego-psychological considerations begin to make themselves felt. As a rule the artistic attitude in the artist is pitted against the aesthetic attitude in the audience, which is inimical to it. Hence much of the history of art centers around the battle between the artist and the surrounding culture (Hauser, 1951; Egbert, 1970). This has been especially true in modern times, when for the first time in history (since the Renaissance, roughly) artistic works have been signed, so that people have known who the creator was.

Two factors must be sharply distinguished: the relationship between the ego and the id, and the relationship between the ego and society. Both are important, and both play a role in the final productivity of the artist.

ART AND "NEUROSIS"

Much has been written about the relationship between art and "neurosis." Historically the artist has been seen as either a genius or a madman. Neither, of course, is true. The artist is a human being, just like any other human being, but he is able to use certain special gifts (which, under some cultural conditions, he may not even have). On the present-day scene more often than not the neurotic elements in the individual's makeup inhibit his artistic productivity, as they do everything else in life. Yet sometimes it is precisely his own suffering as conveyed to other people that makes him so great; the prime example is Van Gogh.

Art is both communication and expression. These two facets of the artistic process must be kept separate.

INNER AND OUTER CREATIVITY

Two forms of creativity can be distinguished: inner and outer. In inner creativity—seen most clearly in the growth of the child—what counts is the growth process. The child sees something new, though it is old hat to everybody around him. In this form of creativity expression is the major need.

In outer creativity the artistic product says something new to the outside world. This is the creativity of the professional artist, or expert in any field (a "creative" idea). Here there are other problems connected with the creative process.

1. *Inner creativity* is essentially unrelated to the achievements of others. The veriest tyro in painting can go through a creative growth process that is far more significant to him than a brilliant masterpiece by Picasso. Dewey takes this point of view in his attitude toward art: "art as experience."

Ideally the analytic process is one of inner creativity. It is a continued growth toward the ultimate goals of maturity, love, and work.

Inner creativity is within everybody's reach. Since it is not connected with achievement as such, it is growth related to the person's own potential. It is as a rule more gratifying than outside achievement, which always has an element of competitiveness about it.

2. *Outer creativity* is more related to communication and the ideas of others. It is this that is the bugaboo of every artist. How good is it? What contribution will it make? These are the questions that plague every professional artist. Is the jury biased? Is a masterpiece overlooked? Is the publisher turning away another Hemingway?

Outer creativity, inasmuch as it is a form of social communication, requires a strong ego. It is not just an outpouring of the id, as inner creativity may be; it has to say something to other people. It is here that the ability of the artist to use a complex symbol that will mean many things to many people comes into play.

Frequently there is a conflict between inner and outer creativity. The artist learns a certain technique, masters a certain message, and continues to convey that message to the world. He need not necessarily grow. He has found out what he wishes to say, says it, and continues to say it. Eventually time passes him by when the needs of the audience change.

NATURE OF GREAT ART

The question has often been raised: What makes for great art? Art that lasts has the capacity to move audiences in many countries and at many times. It must therefore appeal to something that is pretty basic in human nature. It need not come as too much of a surprise when we discover that some of the essential unitary elements in great literature are the essential conflicts in the Oedipal situation—Shakespeare, Dostoevsky, Sophocles. Should the family constellation change, these dramas would lose their poignancy.

CLASSICAL AND ROMANTIC ART

A distinction has also been drawn between classical and romantic art. One belongs to the ego, the other to the id. One seeks to immortalize the stable elements, the other to dramatize the sexual.

STUDIES OF ARTISTS

An intimate relationship exists between the artist and his work. *Le style c'est l'homme.* And yet it is extremely difficult to pinpoint this relationship in general terms. All that can be said is that in some way the artist's personality is expressed through his work. But it may be directly or indirectly or by various roundabout routes. The study of this problem has led to a large body of literature.

CHAPTER 10

The Family and Transference

The family is a decisive factor in human existence. It forms the basis of all known societies. It is the social framework within which personality develops.

FUNCTIONS OF THE FAMILY

Inasmuch as the family is the core of all cultural groups, it necessarily serves a multiplicity of functions. The functions themselves do not differ much from one culture to another, but the details and procedures vary widely. A culture can really be defined in terms of the ways in which the family carries out its functions. Six of these may be delineated (Parsons and Bales, 1955): (1) the matrix within which childhood development proceeds; (2) the socialization of instinct; (3) the provision of security; (4) human models for behavior; (5) the link with the wider society; and (6) the internalization of culture.

THE FAMILY AND HAPPINESS

The underlying assumption about marriage is that it provides happiness. The wedding ceremony is a gala affair, and it ends with the promise, spoken and unspoken, that the couple will live happily ever after. Since happiness is hard to measure, it is customarily avoided in empirical work, yet that does not detract from its crucial importance.

Data on the family are available from all parts of the world, and from a variety of historical epochs. Necessarily, the major focus will have to be on the contemporary American family, with varied references to other cultures.

One indicator of happiness is mental health. On this point the evidence is virtually unequivocal. A disrupted society, which means essentially disrupted families, produces a much higher percentage of mentally ill people than a stable, cohesive society. To cite only one study of many, Leighton (1959), after years of study of psychiatric disturbance in the Maritime Provinces of Canada, found that disturbance was high when there were many indices of societal disintegration. These indices were: (1) high frequency of broken homes; (2) few and weak associations and poor communication between members of the community; (3) poor and weak leaders; (4) few and inadequate patterns of recreation; and (5) rampant hostility, crime, and reliance on alcohol and drugs to alleviate suffering.

But while a disrupted society is certain to produce all kinds of mental and emotional disturbances, mere outer stability in the society or the family is not sufficient to guarantee happiness. Even more important than the outer criteria are the inner dynamic questions of the ability to communicate, capacity to love, degree of cooperation, and the like. The family, in other words, is most conducive to happiness as it approaches the image of the analytic ideal.

SOCIAL CLASS AND EMOTIONAL DISTURBANCES

Within our own culture, there is an inverse ratio between social class and emotional disturbance. The classic study along these lines is Hollingshead and Redlich's *Social Class and Mental Illness* (1958). They found a significantly larger proportion of mental disorders in the lower classes, and they found more psychotics and fewer neurotics in the lower classes than in the upper classes. Ten years later, in a follow-up study (Myers and Bean, 1968), the same essential relationships still held: more severe illness in the lower classes, together with more physiological treatment, more custodial care, and poorer prognosis all around. Thus again while the preponderant majority of the lower classes may have maintained the intactness of the family, the emotional climate is so bad that it produces an inordinate amount of suffering and unhappiness.

MARRIAGE AMONG THE AMERICAN ELITE

But statistics tell only a small part of the story. A more intimate picture is obtained by examining lives in detail. Such a study, focusing on the essentials of marriage, was done by the sociologist John Cuber in collaboration with Peggy Harroff (1965). They interviewed a representative group of the leadership echelon, the decision makers, the most clearly successful, as success is currently conceived. In all, there were 235 men and 202 women, aged between thirty-five and fifty-five. Of these, 406 were married, 31 unmarried; of the unmarried, fifteen were divorced, four were widowed, and twelve had never married.

The methodology chosen was the unstructured, lengthy, and intimate interview. Each person was interviewed separately, sometimes by both authors together, occasionally by only one. It had been anticipated that many of the people approached would be reluctant to talk. Cuber and Harroff say that they "could not have been more wrong." There were only two refusals; the rest talked freely and at great length.

Five Life Styles in Marriage

In the enduring marital relationships of those who had never been divorced or even contemplated it, five distinct life styles showed up repeatedly, and the pairs within each of them were remarkably similar in the ways in which they lived together, found sexual expression, reared children, and made their way in the world. These were the conflict-habituated, devitalized, passive-congenial, vital, and total. Obviously only the last two, representing a small percentage of the total sample, approach the ideal of happiness.

Cutting through these five types, they sorted all the marriages into utilitarian and intrinsic. They found that the great majority were utilitarian—marriage was useful, not intrinsic, based on deep love and understanding.

Reflecting on their findings, they speculate about whether they apply to other classes as well, and conclude that they do. In short, they see their typology as applying to all marriages. So the general conculsion about marriage is: happiness is not the usual result; adjustment (utilitarianism) is.

WORKING-CLASS FAMILIES

A study of working-class families was published by Mirra Komarovsky in 1962. Here the question of whether these marriages were happy or not was made explicit from the very beginning. The families were generally stable, respectable, and law-abiding, sharing deeply internalized and common values. Yet one-third were very unhappy, one-third only moderately happy, and only one-third could have been considered happy.

The primary problem with these lower-class marriages was the lack of meaningful intimacy. In fact, Komarovsky says, at one point there was hardly a marital problem that did not point to some psychological strain.

CULTURE OF POVERTY

Another approach to the lower-class family was adopted by the anthropologist Oscar Lewis, who popularized the term "culture of poverty." Most of Lewis' work was done with deviant ethnic groups, either here or abroad. His method was to spend long hours with the families, eliciting all their activities, including moods and feelings. in minute detail. Naturally the results are impressionistic, but grim. The hardships and misery depicted in his books often read like tragic novels (Lewis, 1959).

FAMILY PATHOLOGY

With so many demands made upon it, it is no surprise that the family tends to break down in a variety of ways. With the discovery that schizophrenics come from schizophrenic families came the increasing realization that all disturbances run in families. The individual is neurotic or healthy within a family environment that is neurotic or healthy, so that the idea of a "sick" child in a perfectly "healthy" environment, on the medical model, has been completely abandoned, except for certain rare conditions that are demonstrably organic.

Within the range of families, most attention has naturally been focused on the lower classes, who provide the bulk of the problems that come to the attention of clinics and hospitals, though not, in the larger sense of the word, the bulk of the problems that beset the world. Minuchin et al. (1967) comment that the stereotyped way in which the children they studied related to the surrounding world reflected a quality of experience that seemed to be comprised of several factors: a sense that "the world stimulates me and I am only a passive recipient of stimuli," an either/or experience of aggression without the ability to tune in nuances of affective experience; an accompanying lack of flexibility within an extremely narrow range of verbal response; and a concomitant inability to focus on an event in such a way as to be able to store or, later on, recover the experience. Kagan (1961) found that the intellectual discouragement of the lower classes can be detected as early as twelve months.

But, as the Cuber study and others have shown, there is plenty of pathology in seemingly stable families as well (Handel, 1967). The study of this pathology has already merged with the broader field of psychiatry, so that it really needs no special treatment; rather it serves as a corrective to the narrow approach of Kraepelinian psychiatry. Perhaps most worthy of mention is the study of the struggle for power within the family. Persons called "neurotic" or "psychotic" in our culture are frequently the result of scapegoating within the family (Ackerman, 1958; Handel, 1967).

ALTERNATE FAMILY STYLES

Because of the widespread incidence of family pathology, many have suggested that the problem lies within the family per se. There is some rationale for this view, since as an institution the family simply has too many demands made on it. But how this should be changed is another matter.

Many cultures with more extended families than our traditional nuclear family have been described. But no one has yet shown that a mere extension will lead to a substantial increase in happiness without a concomitant inner change.

COMMUNISTIC EXPERIMENTS

The nineteenth century was preeminently the time of communistic experimentation in this country. Nordhoff, in his classic study *The Communistic Societies of the United States* (1875), has described the major experiments. Some were completely free sexually, some completely abstinent. Other variations existed. All these experiments failed; the communistic societies of the past century have all but disappeared. Sooner or later, apparently, human passions disrupted the smooth flow of the attempt to establish an ideal community.

Communes have again become prominent since World War II (Fairfield, 1972). Almost all of these are sexually free, propagandizing a form of group marriage which can be conducted in a secluded spot or within the confines of a large city. None of these communes has lasted very long, so that a final judgment on them must wait.

THE PSYCHOANALYTIC ALTERNATIVE

It is to be noted that the image of the psychoanalytic ideal also provides an alternate family style, but one guided by inner rather than outer change. Sociopsychologically, the argument is that family pathology comes from excessive hostility, rather than from the extreme demands made on it. Both scapegoating and power struggles, which lead to so much overt suffering in our culture, are examples of hostility.

Further, the family as now constituted offers certain undeniable advantages. The nuclear family, as Murdock (1949) has shown, is universal, indicating that it gratifies some deep inner need in mankind. Love begins within the family; it is the mother whom the child must first love, not mankind in general. What seems to be needed is rather a loosening of prohibitions on the family structure rather than a mechanical change. When that is done, in line with the image of the analytic ideal, the results may well be dramatic for mankind.

TRANSFERENCE AND HUMAN RELATIONSHIPS

BROAD SIGNIFICANCE OF TRANSFERENCE

Although transference was discovered in connection with therapy, as a result of which it is generally connected with that area, it applies far more broadly. As Freud wrote (vol. 20, p. 42), transference is a universal phenomenon of the human mind, it decides the success of all medical influence, and in fact dominates the whole of each person's relations to his human environment.

By transference is meant the carry-over of childhood interpersonal attitudes toward present-day interpersonal relations. In and of itself, this transference is neither good nor bad; it is a fact of human nature. What gives transference its neurotic cast is its unconscious compulsive character, which prevents the individual from exercising rational judgment in his handling of his interpersonal relationships. It is important to remember that transference as such can lead to happiness as well as to unhappiness.

TRANSFERENCE AND IMPRINTING

In recent years the phenomenon of imprinting has made a considerable impression on psychologists, and in many cases is compared with or seen as the basis of the transference phenomenon. This is a superficial analogy, though the fact itself is of considerable interest. In imprinting the young animal attaches itself to an older animal or human being (this latter is extremely important), from which it never again wishes to detach itself. This imprinting can occur only when the animal is quite young; at later ages the patterns are too fixed to be altered. What is particularly striking is the way in which the young animal can attach itself to a human being (Lorenz, 1963).

However, this is a somewhat different phenomenon from transference. In transference there is attachment to a parent figure that is internalized. This introject (later superego) colors decisively the interpersonal relationships the person forms, but one should not expect, nor does one see too often, a simple one-to-one correspondence.

It is the internalized character of the transference introject that explains the peculiarly human situation, and differentiates it from the animal.

TRANSFERENCE AND NEUROSIS

Happiness is also the outcome of transference, this time satisfactory positive transferences. Ideally, if the relationship with the parents is a good one, the child grows up, builds a healthy ego on the basis of loving relationships and a series of narcissistic gratifications, then eventually chooses loved ones and friends on the basis of his happy childhood experiences.

Neurotic character structure, while it has many dynamic elements, is maintained primarily by a series of (or one) transference reactions to people; neurosis is a life of neurotic transferences. From this it follows that rational argument is of little avail in the management of people's lives as long as they are ridden by such neurotic transferences. Hence neurosis can also be looked upon as the continuation of maladaptive transferences.

CHAPTER 11

The Superego

Of the three main pillars of the structural theory, the id, the ego, and the superego, it is the superego that is the most novel in historical development. It is indeed a brilliant concept that at one stroke unifies a number of otherwise disparate mental phenomena and offers the most useful bridge available to the clarification of man's social and moral values.

The superego can be defined most simply as the internalization of the parents. It is also referred to as the unconscious conscience, but that obscures the relationship to the parents. It describes a fundamental aspect of human behavior, the internalization of parental commands and prohibitions. Prior to the formation of the superego, these are external, hence changeable with the parents. Once it is formed, they are internal, therefore no longer changeable.

SUPEREGO DEVELOPMENT

Sometime between the ages of five and six, when the Oedipus complex is being resolved, the superego comes into being. It may be formed somewhat earlier, however, or a little later. Gould in her empirical study (1972) reports on one child who seemed to have some superego formation at the age of two. Others have noted similar phenomena in slightly older children. But five or six seems to be the mean age.

The superego is part of the human being's need for order. The free release of impulse, though it may be momentarily gratifying, is also confusing. Order, command, structure, system—these are just as necessary to functioning.

Precursors of the superego may be seen quite early. From the earliest weeks of life onward, the development of the ego is marked by the construction within the mind of the child of organized frames of reference or schemata which subserve adaptation. It seems preferable to think of an organizing activity to describe the construction of these inner models. Organizing activity begins to occur extremely early in life. Initially the need-satisfying experiences are not differentiated from the self, but as time goes on a distinct mother schema is organized. It consists, in essence, of a set of expectations relating to the mother's appearance and activities. When the mother's behavior does not in fact correspond to the cathected internal mother imago, the child experiences frustration and anger. The internal mother imago is not a substitute for an object relationship but is itself an indispensable part of the relationship.

The needs of the child progress from the need for bodily satisfaction and comfort to a need to feel loved in a variety of other ways as well. The child's many attempts to restore the original narcissistic state provide an enormous impetus to ego development. Two techniques are especially relevant for the restoration of the sense of well-being: (1) *obedience* to and compliance with the demands of the parents; (2) *identification* with and imitation of the parents. Identification with parents and others is a normal process, and by no means always a defensive act.

The development of the superego proper is linked with the resolution of the Oedipus complex. The major source of self-esteem then is no longer the real parents, but the superego. Introjection of the parents has taken place, and a structure has been formed which did not exist in this form before. What distinguishes the introject from the internal schema is precisely the capacity of the introject to substitute in whole or in part for the real object as a source of narcissistic gratification. What is introjected is not the personality of the parents, but their behavior.

Following Freud, some authors argue that the degree to which the hostile wishes cannot find expression through the ego will determine the degree of severity or even savagery of the superego. This may occur to such an extent that the superego may be a much-distorted representative of the real parents of childhood. Others maintain that the severity of the superego corresponds more exactly to that of the parents, except that their severity was exercised primarily in relation to the instincts.

There has been a strong tendency in psychoanalytic writtings to overlook the very positive side of the child's relationship to his superego, a relation based on the fact that it can also be a splendid source of love and well-being. That the reinforcement of identification with the parents is something that occurs concurrently with superego formation and progression into latency cannot be questioned.

That dependence on the superego is so long-lasting and results in more or less permanent changes in the ego is a reflection of the child's dependence on his real parents as a source of narcissistic gain in the earliest years of life. Self-esteem becomes a function of the superego.

CONSOLIDATION DURING LATENCY

The superego, though it begins early in life, is consolidated in the latency period. This fact has been insufficiently appreciated. Actually instead of calling it latency it could more justifiably be called the period of superego consolidation. It is here that the child begins to relate to authority figures and to peers. The ego has developed sufficiently so that this relationship can take place on an internalized and abstract level; at the same time the development is still not so far advanced that the abstractions have real meaning to the child.

In this period the child seeks authority more than anything else. Tell him what to do and he is satisfied. At the same time he rebels against authority, though not nearly to the extent that he does later on, in adolescence.

Why should the human being need an internalized superego in the latency period? First of all, it is the most economical way of functioning: as in so many other psychic activities, to internalize is to make things run more smoothly. Second, it overcomes the fears of the outside world which are such an inherent part of growing up. Without the superego or its equivalents (parents, authority figures) these fears are overwhelming. Hence every society provides some form of authority; without it the society cannot function. And third, the superego acts as a transitional object by which the individual gradually frees himself from the parents. Such transitional objects are noticeable at every stage of development. The human being's attachments are so strong that this is the only way in which they can be broken. Fourth, the superego binds the libidinal and destructive energies that would otherwise disrupt the individual and his society.

It is noteworthy that it does not matter what superego form is chosen: virtually everything has been seen in one form or another in human history. What counts is that there should be an authority that is internalized in the form of a superego. No culture has ever been found which did not permit superego formation.

ADOLESCENT DEVELOPMENT

The adolescents' superego friction arises because of the discrepancy between the stated ideals and the amount of real gratification provided. Adolescent rebellion appears to be a feature of almost all human societies (Kiell, 1964). It is the adolescent's technique for acquiring some individuality and sense of independence in his own right. Also, much of the hostility that has been repressed before now comes out in more or less undisguised form because of the ego's greater ability to cope with it.

However, besides adolescent rebellion there is also adolescent conformity, which is just as strong. The adolescent is still looking for authority, for superego controls. As long as authority offers reasonable gratifications for the instinctual demands, the rebellion does not become excessive. But when the instinctual renunciation demanded is too severe, as has been the case in Western civilization for many centuries, there is a sharp clash between conformity and rebellion. Then two sides emerge in society, the conservative and the revolutionary. The conservatives function by means of an identification with the aggressor; they now wish to occupy the seats of the mighty, to play the same roles in laying down superego strictures that their parents once played with them. The rebellious struggle against authority; they wish to overthrow the representatives of the superego commands. Often enough, however, inwardly they merely wish to take their place; hence so many revolutions end up with a struggle for power, because so many revolutionaries object to the assumption of the superego role by someone else.

In adulthood and old age the superego plays less and less of an essential role. Here the person himself becomes the superego figure; his own superego is in the background. This is of course ideal; in reality the vast majority of people require some authority and some superego all through their lives.

The psychology of the superego helps to explain the fundamental need for leadership in human affairs. Man is a horde animal, not a herd animal. Just as an individual craves parents to help him, so as a social being he craves leadership to help him over his social confusions.

As before, here too the conservative and the revolutionary elements begin to appear.

CLINICAL APPLICATIONS

In the various clinical conditions the concept of the superego has become indispensable as an explanatory tool. The entire theory of the neuroses has had to be rewritten to include it.

In depression the superego punishes the ego because it is not living up to the demands of the ego ideal. These demands are internal, hence no amount of external success can be properly evaluated without knowing what the internal demands are. When these demands are harsh enough, suicide may result.

In mania the superego fuses with the ego and approves of everything that the ego does. Freud compared it to the feast of primitive tribes when they can break all the taboos, the totem meal. What was always forbidden has now become permissible. This is why manic-depressive swings exist in everybody, with the superego alternately punishing and rewarding, even though the psychosis is rare.

In schizophrenia the internalization of the superego is disrupted, and the patient acts as if his introjects were real entities. Sometimes these introjects are projected to real people or entities (persecutors or TV sets). Sometimes boundaries are lost and the individual can no longer clearly see the difference between himself and others; this represents a symbolic fusion with others, originally mother. Because of the fluidity of projections to the outside world, normally repressed, the behavior of the schizophrenic becomes more unpredictable.

In obsessional neurosis the patient is suffering from a harsh superego. The regression from love to hate which Freud had noted can be better understood as the internalization of the punitive parents. This helps to explain why obsessional stages and schizophrenia are so close: the superego differs only in degree; genetically the parental frustrations differ only in degree.

In hysteria the superego is relatively mild, and is fairly easily placated. This is why the hysteric tends to respond to treatment so readily, especially the hysterical woman: the analyst is her father-superego, and if she can please him her problems are solved.

ASPECTS OF THE SUPEREGO

Certain features of superego functioning are particularly important for all psychological theory. These are (1) internalization, (2) variability, (3) projectability, and (4) confused perception of other people.

1. *Internalization* has already been discussed. It is because there is an internal psychic control that it is so difficult to change the human being.

2. *Variability* reflects the ups and downs of parental control. Few parents are harsh all the time. As a rule they punish, then let go, then reward, and then the cycle is repeated. This is reflected in the fluctuations of the superego. The ordinary mood swings of everyday life are due to these superego fluctuations.

3. *Projectability* means that the superego is projected to other people. This is especially noteworthy in authority figures, marriage partners, and the psychoanalyst; it can even be done with the parents, which creates such a conflict in the teenager.

4. *Confused interpersonal perception* results from these constant projections. Where there is greatest projectability, as in the schizophrenic, relations with other people may become altogether impossible.

CHAPTER 12

Identity, Identification, the Self, and Narcissism; Group Behavior and Experience

THE SENSE OF IDENTITY

The question of identity has become one of the burning conflicts of our age. People come to analysts looking for a "sense of identity," national symposia are held on the topic of our identity as a nation. Alienation, or the absence of identity, is seen everywhere as one of the root causes of emotional disturbance.

Although the concept of identity originated with and was developed by analytic authors, the student who approaches the subject is quite apt, as Roy Schafer says (1968, p. 2), to be bewildered if he tries to make sense out of everything that he reads. The major reason for this bewilderment is that Freudian authors in discussing the topic have as a rule omitted or underplayed the role of social factors, while non-Freudian authors have tended to underplay the role of individual and libidinal factors. Both aspects are essential (Abend, 1974).

Various terms have been used by various authors, and their discussions often seem to cover different ground. This disparity exists largely because each person has tried to erect his approach into a total system without paying sufficient attention to other phases of the problem.

The terms "identity," "identification," "self," and "narcissism" all cover similar ground. Identity and self-image may be used synonymously. Identification (with its forestages of incorporation and intro-

113

jection) and narcissism have to be scrutinized in relation to the experience of identity. The crucial questions to be answered are: (1) How does the individual's identity arise? and (2) How does it integrate with the individual's life and happiness?

THE SEPARATION-INDIVIDUATION PROCESS

Originally the infant has no separate sense of identity; it must develop gradually. Initially there is a fusion with the object, or a symbiotic state (Mahler). The first symbiosis is with the mother. Out of this the child begins to separate sometime in the first year of life. Through a series of steps (hatching, practicing, rapprochment, object constancy) it reaches a stage where there is a fairly clear sense of self and of the other person. This is the stage of libidinal object constancy, where some internalized image of the other person can be maintained, thereby facilitating interaction.

This separation-individuation process provides a paradigm for all later development. Individuation proceeds to a point where there is a period of self-consolidation involving attachment to some other person. From there it then goes on again to separation from the person (or internalized image) and eventual individuation. Thus the attainment of a sense of the self is never a simple process attained overnight.

HEALTHY AND PATHOLOGICAL NARCISSISM

Narcissism is self-love. The course of life involves a balance between narcissistic gratification and gratification with others. Which side of this balance will prevail, as well as the degree of the balance, depends on the vicissitudes of the relationship with the parents.

Narcissism may be either healthy or pathological (Federn). Healthy narcissism arises out of a healthy sense of self-love, which in turn derives from a positive series of experiences with the parents, who explicitly or implicitly encourage the child to grow in an independent manner. Pathological narcissism is a reaction to the clinging possessive attitudes of the parents, who will not allow the child to separate.

Naturally this scheme is a purely ideal one. In practice narcissism arises on a secondary basis in response to the pressures from the early milieu. Sometimes it acquires a secondary autonomy, as in artists and scientists, which leads to constructive activities, often of the highest order. At other times it remains tied to the parents, serving a purely defensive function of isolating the individual from their critical blows or views (the harsh superego). This is the daydreaming kind of child who escapes into a world of his own to avoid parental disapproval. In still other cases there are mixtures in varying degrees of the two kinds of narcissism.

PSYCHOTIC, NEUROTIC, AND NORMAL IDENTIFICATIONS

Identification per se may run the gamut from the reasonably healthy to the completely psychotic. In the psychotic, which is the most striking, there is a total denial of reality. Such a psychotic identification is the last stage of a long process of successive withdrawals from human interaction; it is the expression of a deep sense of despair about ever achieving any meaningful gratifying experiences with other human beings. The sequence that Bowlby describes in response to maternal loss in childhood, protest, despair, detachment, may be seen as the one which leads to such a morbid result. Detachment may continue, or be defended against, by some peculiar identification. Since it arises out of deep disappointments, such a self-image cannot be altered without rearousing some of the intense anxiety previously suffered. Hence it is defended with the utmost tenacity.

The process of reaching identity involves first incorporation, next introjection, and finally identification. In the psychotic there is a halt at incorporation of the parental images. Hence he also shows a marked and bizarre distortion of the body image. The earliest experience with the bad breast leads to a distortion of the body image which grows more apparent as time goes on.

Neurotic identification differs only in degree from the psychotic, yet naturally the degree is important. However, many seemingly intact personalities hold on to a self-image that has many bizarre qualities, and which is refractory to anything but the most intense long-term analysis. Such, e.g., is the persistent feeling of being a failure.

In normal identification the modeling on the parents has a highly positive quality to it. The child imitates various of the parental activities, for which he receives approval from them. Eventually this series of imitative behaviors is internalized as an identification (Meissner, 1974) which in turn meets with the same benevolent approval from the superego that the child once received from the parents. A series of such identifications in an ideally organized society would lead to the normal repetition of the life cycle of the culture. Clearly that has rarely happened in human history, yet as an ideal it remains important.

GROWTH AND IDENTITY CRISES

As a result of the maturation of the various libidinal zones, the growth process involves a dramatic change in the self-image at various phases in development. For these Erikson has coined the apt term "identity crises."

The notion of a crisis highlights the widespread changes that occur at different periods in development. Consequent on each new libidinal phase there is an extensive restructuring of the self-image to account for the novel experiences. This restructuring has many different aspects to it. As before, it follows the symbiosis (or anaclitic) separation-identification paradigm. If the new urges can be incorporated into the self-image, eventually the person goes on to a new stage of individuation; if not, he falls back into one or another of the many defensive postures that make up so much of human life.

The crisis aspect of identity change has been discussed most fully in connection with adolescence, where torment, conflict, despair, and rebellion are most apparent. It is in adolescence too that the child is for the first time able to choose from many alternative models provided by the culture in opposition to what his family has set out for him. Hence a new identity crisis arises for the parents, occasioned by the growth of the child, and they too must go through an extensive restructuring of their world.

By their very nature crises cannot last indefinitely. Consequently once the crisis is resolved by the formation of a new identity, the self-image acquires considerable stability, for fear of falling back into the old turmoil. This is one of the major factors accounting for the tenacity with which people can hold on to seemingly absurd descriptions of themselves.

Because of the restructuring required, the libidinal phases pose serious threats to the equilibrium in many individuals. Not surprisingly, at every stage there are numerous breakdowns, as at the inception of school (Oedipal phase), shifting from one school to another, puberty, marriage, parenthood, and so on. Often these breakdowns are handled by regression to some former identification; e.g., in the postpartum psychosis the most common delusion is that the girl has become a virgin again. Here too the guilt attached to the new identification is readily apparent.

CULTURAL MODELS FOR IDENTIFICATION

The child is largely confined to the models provided by the parents. Once adolescence is reached a far wider choice is possible in more advanced cultures. Nevertheless there are many pressures leading to a decision in favor of one or another of the models available. Certain models are strongly emphasized by each culture, e.g., the warrior, the businessman, the housewife, the emanicipated woman, etc. In each of these there are common elements, so that a basic personality structure (Kardiner) arises for each culture. This basic structure, though applicable to only a limited percentage of the members of the culture, plays a predominant role in the psychic structure of the entire culture. The reciprocal interaction between psychological factors and the culture is so profound that the statement is justified that civilization is a form of psychohistory.

In less advanced cultures the number of available models is generally smaller than in more advanced ones. Such a lack of choice has both positive and negative features. In its most positive form it is found in cultures where the identification with the parents is direct and gratifying. In its most negative form it leads to a passive acceptance of "fate," which serves as a mask for deep despair.

ASPECTS OF THE SELF

A number of other aspects of self and identity formation and function have been discussed at length. Among the most important of these are the following:

1. *Body image.* The self-image begins with awareness of bodily sensations and is always strongly influenced by them. The differentiation of body from mind is an important milestone which the individual attains only gradually, and then with numerous reservations; the capacity to make the differentiation is an index of mental health.

In the earliest, oral stage, when separation anxiety predominates, the infant has a variety of fantasies of bodily destruction, which may persist in various forms. Secure mothering serves to diminish these fears.

In the Oedipal period the first sharp clear-cut sexual differentiation occurs, though in some cultures it is artificially forced earlier. In the boy this arouses castration anxiety, the management of which leads to various personality formations (Alexander, 1923), such as the masochistic (submission to father) or the phallic-narcissistic (rebellion against father). In the girl the major psychic reaction is penis envy, which may be handled by vindictiveness, wish fulfillment, or submissive identification with mother. Both castration anxiety and penis envy are culturally determined manifestations, the severity of which varies with the attitude of the culture toward sexuality. The consequent identification as man and woman, which eventually comes out of these conflicts, and is also primarily culturally determined, always remains a primary element in the self-image.

2. *Internationalization.* The development of an introject begins early in life (three months on), though it is not really consolidated until the superego stage (five to six years). As a result of internalization processes the individual becomes increasingly refractory to outside influences, and increasingly dominated by his inner life. Surface descriptions of identification are consequently often misleading, covering up the deep unconscious identifications that can be elicited only by careful research.

3. *Self-awareness.* The degree to which any person is aware of his "true" self depends on age, level of intellectual development, and degree of disturbance. In all except rare individuals the capacity is limited to varying degrees.

4. *Superego regulation.* The self-image centers between two extreme poles: self-aggrandizement and self-effacement (selflessness of the mystics). Both of these represent unworkable defensive postures. The goal of therapy becomes a correct awareness of the person's real self, and appropriate efforts to change in a philosophically desirable direction.

6. *The inner self and the social order.* As a rule there is a considerable discrepancy between the inner image of the self and the outer self displayed to the culture. This discrepancy is particularly obvious to the practicing psychotherapist because he deals with it all the time. Anthropologists and other social scientists have paid insufficient attention to it, perhaps because the measuring tools at their disposal are inadequate. A social role can be maintained which is at an enormous distance from the inner self, though much conflict will then result.

7. *Alienation* occurs when a person is frustrated with the social role imposed on him either because of excessive demands of the society or a lack of gratification of inner needs, or both. Alienation may be viewed as one measure of the stability of a social order. However, in a disordered culture alienation may actually be an advantage, as the example of the Hutterites in our own society shows (Eaton and Weil, 1955).

IDENTIFICATION AND GROUP BEHAVIOR

The division between the individual and the group occurs for purely theoretical purposes; neither one exists without the other, and neither can be properly understood without reference to the other.

DEVELOPMENTAL PATTERNS

Since family and group are so close, a developmental analysis is bound to be helpful. To begin with, the individual must at some point in his life differentiate himself from his family of origin. This raises the question of the psychological meaning of kinship, which has baffled anthropologists for more than a century, leading to a host of rival theories. Most plausible seems the position of Fortes (1969) that kinship is associated with rules of conduct whose efficacy comes, in the last resort, from a general principle of kinship morality that is rooted in the familiar domain and is assumed everywhere to be axiomatically binding. He calls this the principle of *kinship amity,* which has also been called prescriptive altruism, or the ethic of generosity. Kinship, in other words, is an institutionalized way of expressing affection. The proverb "Blood is thicker than water" expresses this idea pithily.

Although the old evolutionary idea that humanity was once bound together by blood ties that were then replaced by higher forms of social life has been exploded, it is nonetheless true that the individual has to liberate himself from his blood ties and that this liberation occurs in varying degree in different cultures. Blood feuds, in which the individual is lost sight of in the context of some image of "race" or "tribe" of people joined together by common blood, have existed from time immemorial and still exist today, a tragic testimonial to the inability of the individual to achieve such liberation.

GROUP FORMATION AND THE SUPEREGO

In our own culture, ordinary group formation does not take place until the superego has been formed and crystallized to some extent. Thus the early nursery school groups have little lasting meaning to the child; the parents are still more important, because there is as yet no superego. School attendance at six years is made possible by the projection of a now internalized superego to the teacher, who cannot be too different from the parents if the school experience is to be successful. It is not usually until about the age of eight that the superego is sufficiently internalized and sufficiently powerful to propel the child into group formations that are of real libidinal importance. It will be recalled that it is at this age too that the libidinal ties between brother and sister become so strong that social measures have to be taken to restrain them. The first peer groups in our culture are almost always single-sexed, which fits in with the brother-sister avoidance practiced in our culture.

PEER GROUPS

In reference to the significance of peer groups, a paper by Anna Freud and Sophie Dann (1951) reports on a revealing "experiment of nature" which shows that a satisfactory superego can be built up, if nesessary, through a peer group, even though the usual adult figures are absent.

It may be noted also that one of Harlow's findings (1974) was that with monkeys deprived of normal mothering, peer contact was sought out as a substitute, and offered more basis for growth than a substitute object for a mother alone.

Thus peer groups, if formed very early, may lead to the formation of a joint superego that is mutually beneficial to all the members.

In the by far more usual case, where peer group membership becomes emotionally meaningful and socially available to children from the age of eight on, those children who are unable to engage in peer activities, or have difficulties in doing so, will as a rule develop other personality problems later on in life. While superficially group membership before puberty seems less important, and is often played down by parents and teachers, longitudinal studies show that this notion rests on a misconception. Roff and Ricks (1969) identified adults who had child-guidance clinic records and defined their adult mental health status in terms of military information. Culling through the files of the clinics, they rated peer relationships in childhood on the basis of the case history. Regardless of the specific outcome, the consistent finding was that between two-thirds and three-quarters of the individuals with psychiatric difficulties at the time of contact with the military had histories of poor peer relationships. In a control group the incidence was only about one-quarter. Other studies have yielded similar results.

PREPUBERTY GROUPS

Inasmuch as prepuberty groups are almost always one-sexed, the unconscious problem of the maladjusted child would most likely be excessive or premature homosexuality. Using Bion's (1959) classification of group behavior into the three categories of fight, flight, and pairing off, these children would seem to want to pair off prematurely, leading to rejection and isolation because the other children are not ready for it. Collective group action is not yet too significant at this stage, because an adult leader is still essential.

A further important question arises with regard to the socialization of hostility. Groups will frequently turn against other groups, thus forming an in-group vs. out-group battle even within a larger organization that is apparently quite homogeneous, such as a school or a camp. The isolated child is hostile to the group, while the group in turn is hostile to him (or her), using the child as scapegoat. In this way the hostility of the group member is transferred to the group superego, and he is given permission for release which would otherwise be denied to him. In practice it becomes a matter for research to determine how much of a group's cohesiveness is due to the deflection of hostility outward, with the consequent advantage that gives to the member's superego, and how much to the spirit of comradeship and cooperation which appears to be present on the surface.

ADOLESCENCE AND GROUP FORMATION

With the advent of puberty, when the superego is fully crystallized, the ego is strong enough to give the adolescent real freedom to leave the family, and the physiological and libidinal changes are so persistent that they force some kind of resolution, group behavior becomes as vital to the individual's welfare as individual behavior. Indeed, a consideration of adolescent behavior without reference to group experience would be as one-sided and incomplete as one that did not include the operations of the superego.

FUNCTIONS OF INITIATION RITES

In all cultures except certain highly intellectualized sections of our own, adolescence begins with initiation rites. In these rites the pre-adult youths are transformed into full members of the tribe. According to Eisenstadt (1969), this transformation is effected through:

1. A series of rites in which the adolescents are symbolically divested of the characteristics of youth and invested with those of adulthood, from a sexual and social point of view. This investment, which has deep emotional significance, may have various concrete manifestations: bodily mutilation, circumcision, the taking on of a new name or symbolic rebirth.

2. The complete symbolic separation of the male adolescents from the world of their youth, especially from their close attachment to their mothers; in other words, their complete "male" independence and image are fully articulated (the opposite holds true of girls' initiations).

3. The dramatization of the encounter between the several generations, a dramatization that may take the form of a fight or a competition, in which the basic complementariness of various age grades is stressed; quite often the discontinuity between adolescence and adulthood is symbolically expressed, as in the symbolic death of the adolescents as children and their rebirth as adults.

4. The transmission of the tribal lore with its instructions about proper behavior both through formalized teaching and through various ritual activities. This transmission is combined with:

5. A relaxation of the concrete control of the adults over the erstwhile adolescents and its substitution by self-control and responsibility.

To these five functions can be added a sixth: the transition from an adult-controlled group to a peer-controlled one. This transition appears to be more marked among boys than among girls, whose newly created faculty of giving birth leads them more directly to the creation of a new family.

Comparison of cultures that have clearly defined initiation rites with ours produces some useful data. In cultures that have a strong father figure, the initiation of boys at puberty provides a symbolic castration that serves to remind the boys that they are to obey their fathers or suffer the consequences. Some of these rites are so cruel that boys actually die during them. In cultures where there is an absent father (Burton and Whiting, 1969), the boy develops cross-sex identification which is either acted out or, more usually, defended against by exaggerated masculine behavior. It seems that the gang in our culture is an institution with a function similar to that of initiation, and that at least certain types of delinquent behavior are equivalent to the test of manhood in those societies with conflict in sex identity.

With regard to girls, Brown (1969) argues that initiation rites are part of a coherent cluster of customs, and cannot be understood without them. In general, societies that have initiation rites for girls are those in which social stratification is absent, occupational specialization is low, superordinate justice is absent, codified laws are unimportant or absent, individual rights in real property and rules for inheritance are absent, religious specialists are part-time rather than full-time, and sorcery is important. Strong menstrual taboos and male initiation rites are also observed. These generalizations suggest that the rites are part of a set of customs, none of which are characteristic of our own society.

DEVELOPMENT AS A SEQUENCE OF GROUP MEMBERSHIPS

As we move on to the groups that are formed after the physiological events of puberty, with or without initiation rites, we see again that these groups are an essential part of the growth process, which cannot be understood without reference to them. In fact, it would appear that just as the individual moves from one libidinal relationship to another in the course of his life, he also moves from one group relationship to another; this group development has been studied much less than the individual.

Although the image of youth in revolt is a universal one, statistical examination indicates that it is applicable to only a small percentage of the youth in our society (Sherman, 1969; Keniston, 1967). The issue depends on the degree of identification with the parents. Those who identify positively form positively toned groups; those who rebel form negatively toned groups.

POSITIVELY TONED GROUPS

Studies of positively toned groups in our own culture have generally clearly demonstrated the functions that these groups serve in the development of the adolescent. The major ones are: (1) foster constructive activities; (2) consolidate and project the superego; (3) provide a basis for identification; (4) bind the hostile impulses; (5) bind heterosexual and homosexual libido; (6) promote growth toward individuation.

In both the Hollingshead study of Elmtown (1949) and West's study of Plainville (Kardiner, 1945) it was found that teenagers felt very strong pressures from their parents against making social contacts across class lines. Often, however, the development of more parent-independent subcultures oriented around drugs and folk, soul, or rock music may permit or even encourage cross-class contacts, but if the identification with the parents is positive, that will generally carry the day in the long run over the adolescent rebellion.

IN-GROUP VS. OUT-GROUP: AN ETERNAL BATTLE

It deserves to be emphasized that these positively toned groups involve the formation of in-groups and out-groups which are directly in line with the historical observations. In the famous passage that introduced the concept of the in-group, William Graham Sumner wrote (1906, pp. 12-13):

> The relationship of comradeship and peace in the we-group and that of hostility and war towards others-groups are correlative to each other. The exigencies of war with outsiders are what makes peace inside, lest internal discord should weaken the we-group for war. These exigencies also make government and law in the in-group, in order to prevent quarrels and enforce discipline. Thus war and peace have reacted on each other and developed each other, one within the group, the other in the intergroup relation. The closer the neighbors, and the stronger they are, the intenser is the warfare, and then the intenser is the internal organization and discipline of each. Sentiments are produced to correspond. Loyalty to the group, sacrifice for it, hatred and contempt for outsiders, brotherhood within, warlikeness without—all grow together, common products of the same situation. These relations and sentiments constitute a social philosophy. It is sanctified by connection with religion.

NEGATIVELY TONED GROUPS: GANGS

Negatively toned groups of adolescents have attracted much more attention than positively toned groups. Even linguistically these two sorts of groups are differentiated: negatively toned groups are referred to as "gangs." The first published sociological study of the gang was Thrasher's classic work, *The Gang* (1926). Since then a number of other studies have confirmed and refined his conclusions. These groups or gangs are characterized by feelings of alienation, instability, distrust, and outbursts of violence. Yablonsky (1970) calls them "near-groups."

GROUP ACTIVITIES AMONG ADULTS

Once the person's development is completed, marriage and a new family become the dominant core around which his life revolves. The family has been called the primary group, others secondary. The question then arises of the relationship between the various secondary groups found in society and the primary group.

FAMILY AND SOCIAL NETWORK

In her seminal work *Family and Social Network* (1957) Elizabeth Bott has demonstrated a fundamental connection between the family and the larger social grouping. Her thesis is that the degree of segregation in the role relationships of husband and wife varies directly with the connectedness of the family's social network. In other words, the more intimate the husband and wife are, the less they move out to other groups; the less intimate they are, the more they do so.

RITUAL AND EXPERIENCE

All human behavior lends itself to ritualization, but group behavior particularly so, since the group per se is more interested in conformity of behavior with its rules than in the special experience of its members. Mary Douglas (1970) has made an exceptionally good point in stressing the reciprocal relationship between these two.

This reciprocal relationship becomes especially clear in the history of religion. What begins as a divinely inspired form of revelation and inner light soon turns into a series of rituals, the performance of which becomes of the highest importance to the established clergy. Revolts against the dominant theology almost invariably begin by attacking the rituals, which have become empty forms.

A similar process can occur in all groups. As a result, alienation from the current social values often takes a set form: a denunciation not only of irrelevant rituals, but of ritualism as such; exaltation of the inner experience and denigration of its standardized expressions; preference for intuitive and instant forms of knowledge; rejection of mediating institutions; rejection of any tendency to allow habit to provide the basis of a new symbolic system.

In its extreme forms, Douglas argues, antiritualism is an attempt to abolish communication by means of complex symbolic systems. It is a viable attitude only in the early, unorganized stages of a new movement. After the protest stage, once the need for organization is recognized, the negative attitude to rituals is seen to conflict with the need for a coherent system of expression. Then ritualism reasserts itself around the new context of social relations. After a while the demands of inner experience again make themselves felt, and the whole process starts all over again.

GROUP MEMBERSHIP AND MENTAL HEALTH

One of the most important of all defense mechanisms is the submergence of the individual within a group. From time immemorial all cultures have adapted this process to the needs of healing (Almond, 1974). The individual can lose himself entirely, as in the army or church, affirm his old self, as in a family-run business or enterprise, or acquire an entirely new self, as in religious conversion or emigration to a foreign country. The emergence of many forms of group therapy marks the adaptation of this principle on a more conscious and hopefully more scientific scale (Rosenbaum and Berger, 1975).

From this point on considerations of group behavior merge into the larger question of social cohesiveness, which will be discussed in Chapter 15.

CHAPTER 13

Adolescence and Later Development

TERMINATION OF CHANGE

Although changes go on all through the life cycle, physiological development is essentially complete by puberty. Physiological completion is accompanied by a certain degree of psychological completion. Once the character structure is formed, which may be as early as the Oedipal period or may be deferred until the onset of puberty, later experiences are strongly colored by transferences from the earlier time of life.

Freud's thesis, never stated with entire clarity, seems to have been that character structure was essentially complete by the age of five. Other analytic authors have extended this; thus Hartmann, Kris, and Loewenstein (1946) allow for changes in the superego and other psychic instances during the latency period. As internalization increases with age, there is less and less likelihood of any real inner change resulting from external forces; and left to themselves, inner structures remain essentially unchanged.

To many this has been a disheartening revelation, and it has often been challenged. The evidence, while very scattered and largely clinical, supports the contention that much is fixated between birth and five, that some changes occur between five and puberty, but that nothing of any real inner significance occurs after then without some kind of psychotherapy. The same statements can be made about physical and intellectual growth. Growth in all spheres seems to come to a stop in adolescence.

BIOLOGICAL "CLOCKS"

Evidence continues to gather that the human organism, like all biological creatures, is subject to a variety of biological "clocks" (Ward, 1971; Luce, 1971). Rhythms are classified according to the time period in which they oscillate. The best studied rhythm is the circadian, or daily, which has been shown to exist in species as low on the evolutionary scale as the paramecium. Other rhythms studied have been the tidal (twelve hours), lunar (twenty-eight days), and annual (one year).

The biological clocks that determine the onset of puberty come to a head sometime between the tenth and fifteenth years, to use the outside limits; eleven and fourteen would encompass most cases. The growth changes in that period are so staggeringly dramatic that certain manifestations in response to them seem almost universal. First, the individual realizes that his growth has reached maturity; this realization comes from comparison with the parents and other ancestors. Since growing up has always been so important to the child, the fact that growth has now come to a halt forces a total reevaluation of his life situation. Second, the bodily changes that occur are equally staggering and dramatic. Most significant, of course, are the sexual: the sex organs come to life, so to speak. Both sexes emit fluids that they had never emitted before, and both realize that they are now for the first time in their lives capable of reproduction. Third, the social changes involve, in varying degrees depending on the culture, the possibility—again for the first time in their lives—of full independence from the family of origin.

DEFENSES IN ADOLESCENCE

In the second separation-individuation conflict, as Blos calls it (1962), the parents play as significant a role as in the first. Seductive actions by both parents and children occur with great frequency, usually accompanied by strong denials all around. Actual incest no doubt indicates severe ego weakness on the part of either parent or child or both. But the conflict is always intense, thereby calling forth a variety of defense mechanisms. Among the various possibilities: asceticism, withdrawal, promiscuity, group membership, infantilization (schizophrenia), outbreaks of violence, and growth toward love.

As Norman Kiell has shown (1964), these are among the universal reactions of adolescence, which have been found in many different cultures.

(a) *Asceticism.* One reaction to the strong sexual urge is to deny it. Often this is accompanied by a glorification of an ascetic way of life. At times this may be institutionalized, as with monks or nuns, or it may be rationalized, as in the YMCA "take a cold shower" advice, which stresses the allegedly harmful effects of masturbation and intercourse.

(b) *Withdrawal.* Withdrawal may be either physical or psychological. Escape solutions are common in adolescence. Because of the ease of travel in modern times, it often takes the form of running away from the immediate environment. This is a device to escape from the superego, which is equated with the parental surroundings.

Equally common is the withdrawal into fantasy. Such a retreat may take many forms. Extreme bookishness and intellectualization is one. Many adolescents remain eternal sophomores. Another is an overemphasis on work. A third alternative is excessive daydreaming.

(c) *Promiscuity.* At the opposite pole is the adolescent who cannot control his or her desires, becoming promiscuous. As a rule, promiscuity is accompanied by a lack of gratification; insatiability is a salient feature of the sex life. There is also an absence of tender feelings, sexual partners being regarded as so many interchangeable objects. The dynamics of prostitution in the girl are quite directly related to the wish to get even with father for not gratifying her sexually (Oedipal revenge).

(d) *Group membership.* A strong push toward group formation is always noticeable in adolescents. It becomes a neurotic solution when the peer values become more important than any rational consideration of the sexual problem. Groups may be completely promiscuous, as in teenage sex gangs, or completely abstinent, even self-castrating, as in the Russian Skoptzi sect. Maintenance of group membership becomes more important than sex as such.

(e) *Infantilization* (schizophrenia). The sex conflict may be avoided by a severe or total regression to childhood. Historically this has been called dementia praecox, or premature senility. More correct would be prolonged infantilization. The child is too frightened to leave the security of the parents. At times this may appear to be simple immaturity, the namby-pamby type. Pushed further, or prolonged too long, it can become a full-blown schizophrenia. Unconsciously, the amount of real permission given by the parents to separate plays a central role in this syndrome.

(f) *Outbreaks of violence.* "If I cannot prove a lover, I will be a villain" were the words that Shakespeare put in the mouth of the Earl of Gloucester. The sado-masochistic patterns of adolescence are strongly tied up with the inability to love. In many cases, sexuality becomes merely an outlet for aggression.

(g) *Growth toward love.* Finally, mention may be made of the normal solution, involving a union of tender and sexual feelings toward a person of the opposite sex. This would derive from a happy resolution of the Oedipal conflict, in which the tender feelings toward the parent are transferred to a person of the opposite sex and combined with the now permissible sexual feelings. Such a solution, though infrequent, is more common than might be supposed.

The problem of the first sex act remains an acute one for the adolescent until it actually occurs. Once it is carried out, its meaning varies widely. In some social classes, such as lower-class blacks, virginity after fifteen is almost unheard of. In others, such as Italian Catholics, the virginity of the girl at marriage, and the double sexual standard of the male, still retain much of their ancient force.

A core conflict for all adolescents is that of homosexuality, which accounts for the intense interest in the topic. Normal heterosexuality is reached at puberty via a homosexual identification with the parent of the same sex. If this identification is a healthy one, it permits the adolescent, like the identification figure, to go further toward a heterosexual choice. If it is an unhealthy one, a variety of homosexual fixations ensue.

Overt homosexuality begins to be crystallized after puberty. The average adolescent will have anxieties rather than give up the heterosexuality. The overt homosexual almost always begins with some heterosexual experimentation, at times even marriage. But then, when the heterosexual anxieties become acute, he gives up the heterosexuality rather than face the anxiety.

Overt homosexuality is never a satisfactory solution, and one seldom finds happy homosexuals. They rely on a variety of pathological defenses to cover up their inner despair.

The first love affair of adolescence plays a crucial role. If it has a happy outcome, which sometimes happens, the person goes on to make a reasonable adjustment. If, as is more often the case, it leads to frustration and rejection, it casts a long-lingering shadow of doubt on all subsequent love experiences. As in the Oedipal period, a successful love affair is necessary to free the adolescent from the parental ties. But the innumerable "crushes" (the word itself is significant) of adolescence show how often this fails, with a variety of deleterious consequences for later development.

(h) *Hostility.* The enormous increase in hostility and violence, so characteristic of adolescence, has been noted from time immemorial. Its major manifestations are adolescent rebellion, homicide, crime, delinquency, suicide, and, in a certain sense, revolution and idealism.

1. *Adolescent rebellion.* The revolt against the parents has been studied in most detail, no doubt because it is most striking. To begin with, however, it must be noted that this revolt is far from universal. Some studies (Bandura, 1973; Blos, 1962) indicate that it is more the exception than the rule. Nevertheless, it is sufficiently widespread to have atracted universal attention (Kiell, 1964; Feuer, 1969).

Most often, rebelliousness occurs as a protest against the parents. It is characterized by chronic nagging and fighting with and defiance of both parents. Often all three are involved in a triangular situation. This behavior goes back all the way to childhood. It soon spreads beyond the family to the school and other authority figures. The child is described by his parents as being always disobedient, though there may be some change during the early grade school years. However, in spite of this behavior, signs of passivity and dependency are readily discernible. These youngsters are often inextricably involved with their parents in their struggles with them, and show very little ability to become even moderately detached from them. They tend to tag along, or even cling to adult teachers or youth workers that they like. Boys may take very quick offense at any threat to their masculinity. Rebelliousness, or the underlying pathology behind it, continues to be a major problem beyond adolescence. In some, rebellious behavior remains as a character trait throughout life; such chronic adolescence is not infrequent. More often the rebellious behavior fades out in middle or late adolescence, and the underlying conflicts about passivity and femininity are exposed. Other forms of masculine protest may take its place, or the underlying passivity may become the predominant manifest personality characteristic.

As gang behavior shows, patterns of conformity are more important than rebelliousness in peer relationships. This contradicts the cliché image of the "psychopath" without a superego. Adults without some superego formation simply are not found.

Social institutions, such as schools, are willing to permit adolescent rebellion within certain limits. Obviously this varies with the culture.

In the present sociocultural environment, during high school rebellion tends to take on a more systematized and institutional form.

2. *Homicide, crime, and delinquency* are among the most important manifestations of adolescent aggression. However, since they are so intimately tied up with the total problem of violence in society, they can best be discussed under the larger topic.

3. *Suicide* is ranked as the second cause of death in adolescence. It is, of course, the result of hostility turned inward. It may be viewed as part of the general malaise in psychopathological behavior attendant upon the realization that no more growth is possible.

4. *Idealism and revolution* are often linked in the adolescent mind. "Down with the old order" is a slogan that appeals to the young, while the contrary wish to preserve the old order is more typical of the old. Insofar as the revolutionary wish is nourished by Oedipal strivings, it represents the wish of the younger generation to overthrow the old (Feuer, 1969). The similarity of complaints and life styles among young revolutionaries in widely differing cultures is quite striking. At the same time, youth is capable of offering new ideas, a fresh outlook, and the energy needed to reform a moribund society. Hence, even if the motivation is Oedipal or neurotic, the social value of revolutionary idealism may still be great.

Wolfenstein (1971) has published a study of three celebrated revolutionaries, Lenin, Trotsky, and Gandhi. In each case he was able to correlate the political beliefs with the experiences with the father. Again, however, such findings should not be generalized too much.

(i) *The identity crisis and the sense of self.* The crystallization of a sense of self in adolescence is the capstone to all previous development. While it has always existed, the actual end to physical growth and the social pressures to pick a way of life that will last for the rest of the person's years force a decision, whether the teenager wishes to reach one or not.

Numerous failures at this point are sufficient evidence of the extreme difficulty of the process. Alienation, or the failure of a sense of identity, has become one of the major critical questions of our time.

LATER STAGES OF LIFE

While much has been written about the later stages of life, theoretically these involve outer rather than profound inner changes. After adolescence no profound personality change can be expected to occur without therapy.

The milestones of later living, such as marriage, parenthood, occupational choice, middle age, grandparenthood, old age, death, mourning, all produce a variety of reactions dictated primarily by the character structure formed earlier in life.

CHAPTER 14

Psychology and the Social Sciences

PSYCHOANALYSIS AS A SCIENTIFIC REVOLUTION

Each scientific revolution, Kuhn points out in his influential work *The Structure of Scientific Revolutions* (1962), alters the historical perspective of the community that experiences it. Psychoanalysis certainly meets the criterion of a scientific revolution. Many will agree that the influence of Freud on the social thought of the twentieth century is comparable only to that of Marx and Darwin in the nineteenth century. No branch of the social sciences has escaped the influence of psychoanalytical ideas.

Yet the manner in which psychoanaysis should be applied to the social sciences is by no means clear, nor is it anywhere clearly stated by Freud or his followers. To reach such a statement is the purpose of this chapter.

THE SOCIAL SCIENCES: DISCORD AND DISAGREEMENT

Two comments may be made about the social sciences. First of all, in contrast to their cousins in the natural sciences, they are shot through with controversies. Almost nothing seems established with any degree of certainty. Unlike the student of physics or chemistry, who is presented with a set of facts reproducible in the laboratory and their explanations, the student of any of the social sciences must wade through a lot of theories, all in sharp disagreement with one another, before he can get to facts, which themselves are in equal dispute.

These controversies have extended to the point of indicting whole disciplines, and castigating their practitioners as apostles of error and futility. Thus in the fields of psychology and psychiatry, Freud threw down the gauntlet in *The Interpretation of Dreams* (1900), stating in effect that anyone who did not understand dreams (which meant virtually the entire profession at that time) should not practice psychiatry. Twenty-six years later in *The Question of Lay Analysis* (1926, p. 230), he repeated his charge that doctors form a preponderant contingent of the quacks in analysis. Sullivan, in *The Fusion of Psychiatry and Social Science* (1964), spoke of many of the contemporary systems of his day as too preposterous to be taken seriously, yet of course the majority of his colleagues did take them seriously. Szasz (1973) deplores the fact that "modern man, with the aid of science and medicine, has developed an especially abhorrent method of controlling his fellow man" (p. 360). Bakan (1967) expressed the feeling that there was a crisis in research in psychology. He deplored the "very poor state of psychological research" (p. xiii). Harlow has commented on the refusal of psychology texts to discuss love. I have argued (1969) that much of experimental psychology is so confused that it has to be discarded; supporting arguments are found throughout this book. Psychological science has to be reconstructed along dynamic lines.

In the field of the social sciences proper, equally caustic comments may be found. C. Wright Mills (Domhoff, 1967) leveled equally bitter attacks on both the academic and the Marxist varieties of social science. Andreski (1972) seriously refers to the social sciences as "sorcery." Phillips (1973) argues that in the light of the faulty quality of many sociological data, the efforts of many sociologists are a waste of time. Gouldner has written a book with the arresting title *The Coming Crisis of Western Sociology* (1972). Dell Hymes (1969) has argued for the "reinvention" of anthropology. In philosophy Kaplan (1961) and Ricoeur (1965) have both urged wholesale reconstruction in philosophy in the light of Freud's revolutionary discoveries. The list could be continued indefinitely.

And second, the social sciences touch upon material that is familiar and politically explosive. The astronomer can search about in the heavens for a new star for several hundred years if he is so minded without inspiring any practical suggestions. But no sooner does the social scientist discover something than he feels, within himself and from others, a call to action. If what he has discovered is more than trivial, it will have immediate application in the sociopolitical realm. If Jensen is right, if blacks are genetically inferior to whites, our entire school system should be changed; if he is wrong, as most social scientists today believe, then the school system should be changed in another way, by giving the blacks a greater opportunity to learn.

THE POLITICAL IMPLICATIONS OF SOCIAL SCIENCE

Politicians have become aware of the profound implications of social science research. Simirenko (1969) reports that in the Soviet Union systematic destruction and persecution of the ablest social scientists in the country began in the 1920s and did not let up until 1938, when most of them had been destroyed. One is particularly struck by the fact that in the 1930s almost all of the museum directors, ethnographers, and archeologists were either arrested or dismissed, never to be heard from again (Simirenko, 1969, p. 12).

In this country social scientists have moved in circles that scarcely touched one another. Analytically oriented psychologists, in the main barred from university positions, gravitated toward private practice, where they concentrated on the direct study of the human being. Experimental psychologists, solidly entrenched in the university hierarchy, devoted themselves to the hypertrivialized study of conditioning reactions which in the main had no appreciable bearing on human affairs.

The battles between warring camps of social scientists have in turn affected government policy. Government administrators, already sorely frightened by what the professors might come up with next, did the only thing that they could do—cut funds. In 1938 the social sciences, in solid with New Deal liberalism, received 24 percent of total government expenditures for research. By 1950 this had diminished to 8 percent, and between 1960 and 1970 it went down further to 3.5 percent to 5 percent (Harris, 1970, p. 3).

THEORETICAL VIEWPOINTS

Although driven by the need for empirical inquiry, the social sciences have historically been dominated as well by broad theoretical viewpoints, sometimes not fully expressed. Prior to Darwin it was the general liberalism stemming from the French Revolution and the history of philosophy. Then with Darwin came the emphasis on evolution, which ruled throughout the latter part of the nineteenth century. Gradually this was replaced by a kind of enthusiastic empiricism, which was sure that if we just accumulated enough facts, all our problems would be solved. Universal knowledge in its turn gave way to the psychoanalytic point of view, which insisted on the primacy of the human being and of unconscious motivation. Finally in more recent years, and in apparent imitation of Einstein's field theory, a structuralist point of view has had the upper hand. Naturally, all kinds of admixtures can be found.

THE IMPACT OF PSYCHOANALYSIS

The impact of psychoanalysis has been enormous but confusing. This confusion stems from three sources. One is that apart from psychoanalysts themselves, no one has really understood the total meaning of Freud's teaching. Second, analysts who set themselves up in opposition to Freud muddied the waters by seriously misrepresenting his ideas (Jung and Adler are good examples). Unfortunately also in later years the very analysts who were most interested in the social sciences, like Fromm and Horney, continued to misrepresent Freud, sometimes even building their own theories on these misrepresentations (Fine, 1973). And third, once social scientists became sufficiently familiar with analytic doctrines, they wanted to practice analysis rather than pursue theory.

Fortunately enough people are available who are familiar with both Freud and the social sciences to build a solid theoretical base. Michel Foucault (1970, pp. 373-65) has correctly seen that psychoanalysis stands in a special position vis-à-vis the social sciences. It is more of a point of view than a doctrine per se; hence it is in a position to exercise a critical function that is absolutely essential to all work in the social field.

This critical function can be defined quite simply as the *introduction of a dynamic psychological point of view*. The social sciences deal with man's behavior in society. Psychoanalysis provides a number of deep insights into the mechanisms of human behavior. With the help of these insights it is then possible to gauge whether the methods of social science are likely to produce meaningful results, and whether the results allegedly obtained really stand up when looked at critically.

THE UNITY OF MANKIND

Man remains the measure of all things, but man as he is revealed to us in all his depth by dynamic psychology, not the robotized man of a superficial associationism. And there is only one kind of man. The myth that the "patient" in analysis is different from his fellow men not in analysis has to be put to rest once and for all. Primitive man and civilized man, ancient man and modern man, black man and white man; Asian, European, and American man; the Colonel's lady and Judy O'Grady; they are all the same under the skin.

To see psychoanalysis as a special discipline (as some psycho-analysts themselves wish to do) is to miss the point. It is rather a matter of applying a broad encompassing theoretical view to the image of man, and then seeing how that works out in the various specialized fields. Such an image cannot be put to any crucial test, any more than can evolution or Marxism or relativity. It can be judged only by its success in integrating a wide range of phenomena from many areas. Mistakes within psychoanalytic theory can be corrected, and are con-stantly being corrected, with little stimulus from the outside. But it is the broad attitude that is really revolutionary.

In discussing the application of that broad attitude to the various specialized fields, what has to be done is to show how the dynamic psychological point of view illuminates the data available, assists us in separating out important from trivial material, helps to build up a methodology for the accumulation of more data, and charts a route for the elaboration of meaningful theories. Though the material is readily available, such a discussion is beyond the scope of this book.

CHAPTER 15

Social Structure: Psychological Aspects

In order to be happy a human being has to find his place within some social order. The recognition of this point of view in one sense provides the most important conceptual change in psychoanalysis since Freud.

CIVILIZATION AS PSYCHOHISTORY

In all the social sciences there seems to have been a shift from more impersonal to more personal forces as the decisive factors in the human being's world. Even in psychoanalysis many of the awesome creatures of Freud's thought, such as the pleasure principle, passivity, the repetition compulsion, the death instinct, have been replaced by more human and more malleable creatures.

One manifestation of this shift is the concept of civilization as psychohistory, which has been gaining ground rapidly in the last few years. Civilizations are now being viewed from a wider as well as a more dynamic perspective, as revealing the unfolding of fundamental patterns of human relationships in the context of those artistic and social forms that embody the manifestations of human consciousness. Civilization, in other words, is what man makes of it. And what he makes of it depends very heavily on how he sees his relationships with his fellow men.

CULTURAL UNIVERSALS AND THE UNITY OF MANKIND

The cultural universals, those features in all known societies, must be restated in more human terms. Kardiner (1939) lists them as follows:

1. They all have some form of *family organization* that can be identified by some formal arrangement among parents and children and members of the extended family. The character of the relations and what constitutes the extended family vary.

2. They all have an *in-group formation* of some kind. The nature and manner of its composition vary.

3. They all have some *larger group*, like clan or tribe, based on family organization, on real or symbolic consanguinity, or on common interests.

4. They all have definite *techniques for deriving sustenance* from the outside world.

5. They all have *basic disciplines;* but what impulses, interests, or needs they control differ widely.

6. They all *control mutual aggression* according to a large variety of standards.

7. They are held together by certain *recognizable psychological forces.*

8. They all create definite and distinctive *life goals* that vary widely and even change within the same culture.

It is within the framework of this basic unity of mankind that the differences among various peoples must be sought. The physical differences among men, as compared, say, with dogs, are small; the range of height, birth, foods consumed, hair colors is relatively narrow. It is in the psychological realm that major variations must be sought.

CULTURAL PATTERNS

Kroeber and Kluckhohn (1952, p. 66) offer this definition:

Culture consists of patterns of and for behavior acquired and transmitted by symbols, constituting the distinctive achievements of human groups, including their embodiment in artifacts; the essential core of culture consists of traditional (historically derived and selected) ideas and especially their attached values.

Within these areas of differences and similarities the individual must find his way in the world into which he is born. It is to be noted how strongly the anthropological emphasis is on the psychic situation.

Chief Justice Oliver Wendell Holmes expressed it more pithily when he said: "Life being action and passion, a man who has not taken part in the action and passion of his epoch can fairly be said not to have lived at all."

SOCIAL CHARACTER (BASIC PERSONALITY STRUCTURE)

In the attempt to formulate the differences among different cultures, the concept of social character or basic personality was developed. Fromm (1941, p. 277) defined social character as a selection of traits; it is the essential nucleus of the character structure of most members of a group that has developed as the result of the basic experiences and mode of life common to that group. Linton, who worked very closely with Kardiner, defined the basic personality type as that personality configuration which is shared by the bulk of the society's members as a result of the early experiences that they have in common (Kardiner, 1945, p. viii).

The notion of a basic personality or social character has come under severe attack from a number of sources (Levine, 1973; M. Harris, 1968). The counterarguments are that human behavior is shaped by the coercive pressures of social survival, involving the maintenance and enhancement of career, reputation, status, and the esteem of others. Hence the environment is more important than the intrapsychic processes. Then there is growing evidence that the basic personality applies to only a small percentage of the population. Finally, there are even some who maintain that the way populations differ psychologically is of little social significance.

These antipsychological arguments miss the point that there are noticeable psychological differences among men, and that the psychological environment in which man lives is shaped by him to varying degrees.

It is true, however, that the basic personality applies to only a part of any group. In one study Wallace (1970) found that a pattern described in a certain Indian population was shared by only 37 percent of the sample tested. Still, this is more than one-third of the group, and remains a significant observation about the group. The question reduces to a quantitative one: how characteristic is the basic personality for any group studied? Answers to such a question would have to shade off from those for whom it is highly characteristic to those for whom it is only peripherally relevant. It certainly seems senseless to throw out the vast mass of data about culture and personality which several generations of social scientists have accumulated because there is more overlap than had been thought, or because the traits described do not last forever under different cultural pressures. Here as so often there seems to be primarily an emotional bias against recognizing the influence of psychological factors in human interaction and in human welfare.

One way to look at the relationship of culture to personality is to think of the psychological world in which each individual lives. Certain aspects of the psychological world are universal, existing for everybody. Others are so private that they may be almost unique. In between lies a vast mass of experiences that are shared mainly by the members of a given culture.

GLIMPSES INTO OTHER CULTURES

With these preliminaries, some of the more important studies in the culture-personality area can be mentioned. The field has become so vast that only a few highlights can be touched.

FROMM'S STUDY OF A MEXICAN VILLAGE

Perhaps the most ambitious study of the psychology of another culture is Fromm's work with a Mexican village (Fromm and Maccoby, 1970). This village had 162 households. All the persons over sixteen and half of the children were carefully studied by special interviews and projective tests (Rorschach, TAT). The results led to the formulation of three major types of social character in the village: (1) the nonproductive, receptive character, the most frequent; (2) the productive-hoarding character; and (3) the exploitative character, which includes two numerically smaller types, the productive-exploitative and the unproductive-exploitative. These three main character types could then be fitted into the socioeconomic background.

PLAINVILLE: THE AMERICAN MIDWESTERN CHARACTER

In his second important work in this field, *The Psychological Frontiers of Society* (1945), Kardiner, in cooperation with James West, published an analysis of the American character pattern as revealed in the Midwest. "Plainville" is a small town in the central part of the United States. The data were collected by Mr. West in 1939-1940 on funds provided by the Social Science Research Council of Columbia University. The field research was done under the supervision of Ralph Linton. Thus this study is more typical of the literature than the previous one: intensive study of a small community by one specially trained individual. Of course, since Plainville is part of the United States, the persons who participated in the full analysis could be assumed to have had some knowledge of the patterns involved.

The analysis, conducted under the leadership of Kardiner, attempted to settle one major and one minor issue: What are the psychological features of Western man, taking Plainville as a base, and second, what are some specific features of Plainville? The general conclusions concern first the basic personality structure without consideration for differences in status, class, or education, and then the breakdown giving due effect to these three factors.

The personality gets a good start and barring the operation of constitutional factors receives a strong underpinning that will support the child in his initial contacts with the outer world and give him practice in eliciting expressive affects. The institutional basis for this is the division of function between male and female, in which the economic load rests on both sexes.

This favorable situation in infancy then undergoes considerable distortion under the influence of later disciplines, which help the process of growth in some aspects but introduce painful factors in others, including some that are highly specific and adventitious. The painful factors are introduced chiefly in the sexual development, that is, in connection with sexual activity of childhood as a relaxer activity. In other words, a marked Oedipus complex.

In connection with sphincter control a new series of events occurs. It is the first training in responsibility and social acceptance under specific conditions. In connection with the evacuating function a series of social values is initiated. These values are obedience, cleanliness, orderliness, and perhaps certain aesthetic values.

One of the consequences of good maternal care is the stimulation of a high degree of curiosity, which, with the aid of a free psychomotor apparatus, leads to the desire to explore, create, invent, and investigate. This aspect of adaptation need not be influenced by the blocked systems created by sexual and other disciplines. It is this freedom of curiosity and manipulative talents that is subject to much training in the form of "education." In connection with educability, large variations exist because of differences in native intelligence, but even more because of the presence or lack of opportunity. The material and intellectual cultures are perpetuated through these channels. However, the opportunities for education are usually accompanied by prolonged dependency on parents, so that this aspect of personality is always developed at the cost of independence, since most "higher education" takes place between the ages of fourteen and twenty-five.

From these constellations in the basic personality structure it is evident that the characterological types emerging from various combinations of operation constellations are very numerous indeed.

Some of the socially relevant outcomes of the basic personality structure can be stressed. Though the emerging individual has a high emotional potential, too many blocked-action systems are created. The capacity for idealization, and hence worship, of "great men" is created, as well as the foundation for a religion with an idealized deity with great power for both good and harm. On the other hand, from the blocked systems we derive (a) serious sexual disturbances, both on the affective and executive side (potency); (b) great variations in aggression patterns, with psychosomatic accompaniments; (c) marked variations in the attitude to authority, excessive submission and passivity (even to the extent of dragging in the sexual organization in the form of homosexuality, asceticism, or perversion); and (d) excessive and premature independence (paranoid personalities). The social relevance of these characterological types is that they contain ferment for social instability.

The struggle for success becomes such a powerful force because it is the equivalent of self-preservation and self-esteem.

The removal of religion as a stabilizing influence in society, despite the persistence of dogma and ritual, was largely due to the increasing knowledge of the outer world and improvements of technique and mastery. These have also contributed to the alteration of the social structure through the introduction of manufacture. With the increased mastery of nature, fewer anxiety situations remained that could be referred to the deity.

The social tensions created by the newer types of organization were not foreseen, and by 1945 a crisis of vast dimensions had been created on that score. The culture is in a state of flux in which many values are changing. For a long time Plainville was oriented on a "feudal" plan in which parental authority had to be augmented because of the paucity of rewards for obedience. The improvement of communication has broken down its isolation, and urban values are gradually seeping in and destroying family solidarity.

Kardiner's trenchant analysis of the American character structure has become an essential part of all American social science. In spite of everything that has happened since, it must still be considered a solid basic piece of research that has been incorporated into larger frames of reference, but not really superseded.

PSYCHIATRIC DISORDER AS AN INTEGRAL PART OF THE CULTURE

One of the major discoveries of modern psychology is that psychiatric disorders are interwoven in the very fabric of a culture. Their recognition, classification, and treatment are as much a part of the "abnormal"; in fact, the very definitions of these terms have undergone wide-ranging transformations. This means that a careful study of what any culture chooses to call "psychiatric disorder" will reveal a great deal of the day-to-day workings of that society (Kiev, ed., 1964).

RÓHEIM'S INTERPRETATION OF THE SEXUALITY OF THE AUSTRALIANS

In 1928 the Princess of Greece, better known in psychoanalytic history as Marie Bonaparte, financed an expedition to central Australia by Géza Róheim. His report, published in a special double number of the *International Journal of Psychoanalysis* (1932), remains one of the classics of psychoanalysis.

Róheim spent several years in the area. He gathered all kinds of material, including dreams, folklore, legends, and play therapy (or the equivalent in Australia) with children. Although the framework of that day was still primarily id psychology, his work represents a gold mine of insights into a primitive people, almost the most primitive ever encountered.

Because of space limitations only the barest outlines of his report can be reproduced here. Róheim subdivided the theoretical section of his paper into the id, ego, and superego; we shall do the same.

The id. Adults as well as children love endless repetition (in our culture this is true of children only). Oral gratification is paramount; the baby sucks whenever it wishes, it is never weaned, and if its own mother is unavailable, some other mother will give suck. Yet these same mothers *kill and eat every other child*. The surviving children are apparently unaffected; they show almost no oral pessimism. However, some anxiety connected with the oral function is projected into the supernatural.

In the anal area they are very free; shame about dirt or even feces or urine is not present. As adults they enjoy the anal aspects of

sexual pleasure, but show none of the reaction formations characteristic of anality in the European or American. Repression on the
whole is very superficial.

The Oedipal situation shows marked hostility toward the father.
This is attributed to the close incestuous ties of the boy with mother.
One of the peculiarities of the sleeping patterns is that the mother
sleeps on top of the child; hence everything is permitted except actual
intercourse. In this cultural group incest excludes seven-eighths of
the women in adult life; Róheim draws a connection between this
wide-ranging incest barrier and the peculiarly close physical tie to
the mother. Castration anxiety is severe later on but in childhood
there are hardly any manifestations of it.

No sign of a latency period appeared. As soon as they can, boys
and girls begin to engage in sex play with one another, including
sexual intercourse.

The ego. The prototypical defense is displacement upward. The
churinga, or bull roarer, which gives off a terrifying roar when it is
swung rapidly, is said to be a totemic object from which children
emanate and into which ancestors are transformed when they die
or sink into the ground. It is a major masculine symbol. No women
are permitted to see a churinga. Róheim sees the churinga as a penis
symbol.

At puberty the boys are subjected to a subincision ritual, which
is quite bloody. This ritual serves to transform direct heterosexual
libido into deflected homosexual libido. For example, in one cree-
mony the men stand around masturbating to the point of erection,
and then let the blood out of the engorged veins. Women are excluded from this ceremony as well. Ceremonial avoidance of the
mother-in-law is practiced, as might be expected from the strong
incest taboo. Projection is a very common defense as well.

In relation to the environment, the native shows more ingenuity
than is commonly supposed. Emotional values attached to the environment are derived from deflected genital libido. Narcissism is also
highly pronounced; girls would gaze at their images in Róheim's
mirror and kiss themselves rapturously. Generally they considered
themselves very pretty, which would fit in with the extensive genital
freedom that they enjoyed.

Nevertheless, they see themselves as leading two lives. One is the
real person, the other the hidden person who has never left the an-
cestral cave and the churinga.

The superego. Before a boy gets his churinga, in puberty, there is very little superego to speak of. Afterward the initiation is a kind of dramatization of repression, or of superego formation. In this initiation ceremony the initiators, symbolic fathers, pour the blood from their veins on the boy's body, after his subincision, which is a symbolic castration. This blood ritual serves to keep the boy always covered with the father's blood.

However, much of the superego hostility is deflected to the outside. When a man dies, it is considered to be the result of witchcraft, and revenge is called for. This revenge is carried out by a young man, who is first required to have intercourse with the dead man's wife; if he forgets or neglects to do so, the woman reminds him of his "duty." Then he gets rid of the superego punishment by killing somebody else.

When the Lutheran missionaries tried to convert the Aranda to the doctrine of original sin, the natives indignantly denied that this applied to them in any way; they said, "The Aranda are all good." There is more real danger in their lives than intrapsychic danger. Róheim sees them as a very happy group of people.

THE EGO AND SOCIETY

CULTURE AND CONFORMITY

Every society exerts, by a variety of means, pressures on its members to conform to certain codes of conduct. There has been a tendency among Western social scientists to deplore this conformity, overlooking or underplaying the fact that it is woven into the fabric of society. Nevertheless, while conformity is expected, cultures allow for deviation within certain limits. The interplay between the conformity and the deviation serves to limit the ethos of any given society.

Group pressures to conform were first designated as "mores" by the sociologist William Sumner. In his classic book *Folkways* (1906, p. 7), he wrote:

> If now we form a conception of the folkways as a great mass of usages, of all degrees of importance, covering instruction for the young, embodying a life policy, forming character, containing a world philosophy, albeit most vague and unformulated, and sanctioned by ghost fear so that variation is impossible, we see with what coercive and inhibitive force the folkways have always grasped the members of a society.

CONFORMITY AND THE SUPEREGO

Parsons (1951) has refined this concept to articulate it with the psychoanalytic notion of the superego. There is a kind of group superego (or more precisely, the group members all have similar superegos), which regulates much of what goes on in ordinary living. It is through this superego that the mores of a culture are transmitted to the young; hence the superego is the link between the individual and the social order.

The pressures of the group upon the individual have been studied largely by sociologists, but unfortunately without adequate reference to the internal reactions of the individual, because they have been primarily interested in phenomena where the reactions of the individual are of secondary importance (cf. Durkheim's definition of a social fact). The reactions of the individual to his instinctual impulses have been studied largely by psychoanalysts, though again frequently without sufficient reference to the social matrix in which they occur. Hence a gap has been left, involving the consideration of the ego's (individual) reactions to group pressures.

Anthropologists have adequately documented the universality of the incest taboo, describing the numerous varieties of the taboo that have occurred in various societies. Psychoanalysts have documented in detail the price that individuals in our society pay for adhering to the incest taboo; by inference a similar price is paid by members of other societies, though it has never been investigated systematically.

There remains the question of the dynamics involved in the individual's reactions to the larger social group. If the ego did not have any reaction at all, everybody would live happily in a state of absolute conformity. If the ego did not have to pay any price for its adherence to the group superego, there would be no suffering. Obviously both of these propositions are untrue, and have never been true in any known society. Hence the relationship between conformity and deviance has to be more carefully examined.

In general, the ego complies with the demands of the culture (parents) in two ways: first by learning to adopt certain roles that are demanded of him, i.e., external behavior, and second by the formation of a superego, which, if in agreement with the societal demands, then stamps them as "correct," "justified," "natural," "divinely ordained," or some other rationalization. Thus the individual forms both external and internal controls. Again, the social sciences have dealt much more extensively than dynamic psychology with external controls, which are much more easily approached from a nondynamic point of view, while dynamic psychology has emphasized the inner controls, attempting to understand them by detailed studies of individuals (case histories).

PRESCRIBED ROLES

The external controls result in the adoption of certain prescribed roles for the individual. As long as he adheres to these roles, the culture tends to leave him alone. By and large the culture is not interested in inner experience; its concern is with the same two factors that go into the formation of the superego: obedience and identification. Like the average parent, the culture is interested only in having the individual do what is expected of him; his feelings about it are pushed to one side.

Yet at the same time cultures recognize that the adoption of prescribed roles should preferably be accompanied by inner feelings of pleasure rather than of resentment. Hence elaborate systems of justification are built up, which become absolute unquestionable dogma to the insider, superficial rationalizations to the outsider. Intellectual arguments about these systems of rationalization, as in religion, are never resolved, because there are weightier issues involved under the surface.

Cultures may prescribe roles for the individual which lead to self-damaging behavior, and even at times to death. As Tennyson wrote in his immortal poem "The Charge of the Light Brigade":

> Theirs not to reason why,
> Theirs but to do and die.

But even if the role prescribed is manifestly inappropriate, the individual finds it hard to rebel. Conformity, generally speaking, is easier, both externally and internally. This would help to explain the well-known conservatism of any cultural group, which tends to perpetuate the same situation generation after generation, century after century.

CRITIQUE OF ROLES: REVISED IMAGES OF NORMALITY

The humanists were among the first to attack the terrible consequences of adhering to the roles prescribed for men in the Middle

Ages. The delusional primitivism of the church-dominated continent of Europe has been so completely eclipsed by the far more awful problems of nuclear warfare and world destruction that there is a strong tendency to forget how bad it was, even to glorify the excesses of that epoch (Parkes, 1970).

In line with their historical derivation from the humanists, the psychoanalysts in the twentieth century have provided an intellectual framework with which to evaluate and criticize the existing cultural traditions. This has led to the widespread self-searching so characteristic of American society, especially since World War II.

One outcome of the psychoanalytic position has been to destroy the older statistical conception of normality. It is no longer possible to see what most people do as "normal" merely because they are doing it. Nor is it possible to regard the average person as mentally "normal"; all the evidence is rather that from an analytic point of view he suffers from many problems, some quite deep. As Freud said at an early stage, he discovered that he had all mankind as his patient.

But if normality is viewed from the standpoint of the analytic ideal, which is the way it should be approached, then man must choose between an adjustment neurosis and a maladjustment neurosis. The adjustment neurosis is another term for the basic personality or the social character; it carries with it, however, the implication that the individual pays a certain price for his conformity to the group mores. The maladjustment neurosis has been studied much more, for obvious reasons. Nevertheless, as has been abundantly shown by now, it cannot be properly understood without reference to the adjustment neurosis prevailing in any particular culture.

THE "NORMAL" MAN

Once it became clear that statistical normality can cover a multitude of sins, the idea of conducting a broad-range study of seemingly "normal" individuals naturally suggested itself, with a view to seeing what they were really like. "Normality" in this sense can be defined simply as an absence of any history of consulting a psychiatrist or any other mental health professional.

The first such study was conducted by a group led by Dr. Thomas Rennie in midtown New York. The results were published in the book *Mental Health in the Metropolis* (1962).

Rennie's group chose a solid area of Manhattan for their study, calling it Midtown. In this area, according to the last U.S. census, lived 110,000 people. They chose a sampling of this number by systematically sampling first all the city blocks, second all the dwellings, and third all the adults between the ages of twenty and fifty-nine. This led to a study population of 1,911 Midtowners in the twenty-to-fifty-nine age range. Of these 1,911, 13 percent turned out to be nonrespondents, leaving a total of 1,660 individuals who were carefully studied by questionnaire and personal interview. Aided by sizable grants, the research went on for a number of years, employing a considerable number of mental health personnel.

In the final classification of mental health status, six categories were used:

1. Well
2. Mild
3. Moderate
4. Marked ⎫
5. Severe ⎬ Impaired
6. Incapacitated ⎭

Although breakdowns by various categories are more significant it is important to note the overall distribution of the ratings. For the entire sample of 1,660 adults it was:

Well	18.5%
Mild symptom formation	36.3%
Moderate symptom formation	21.8%
Marked symptom formation	13.2%
Severe symptom formation	7.5%
Incapacitated	2.7%
Impaired (marked, severe and incapacitated)	23.4%

Thus only 18.5 percent of the adults could be regarded as well enough to be free of psychiatric disturbance, a most surprising and disturbing finding. The authors comment that some may well find their results "staggering in magnitude, and of dubious credibility" (Rennie et al., 1962, p. 139).

Of the various methods of breaking the data down, the most significant was the one with regard to socioeconomic status (SES). By and large, impairment varied inversely with the SES. That is, the poorer the individual, the greater was his degree of mental impairment likely to be.

The authors conclude their study with some suggestions for further research and social reform (p. 236):

> For targeting of social policy, Midtown zones C and D (the poverty zones), and likely their psycho-socioeconomic counterparts elsewhere on the national scene, convey highest priority claims for milieu therapy in its broadest sense. Ultimately indicated here may be interventions into the downward spiral of compounded tragedy, wherein those handicapped in personality or social assets from childhood on are trapped as adults at or near the poverty level, there to find themselves enmeshed in a web of burdens that tend to precipitate (or intensify) mental and somatic morbidity; in turn, such precipitations propel the descent deeper into chronic, personality-crushing indigency. Here, we would suggest, is America's own displaced-persons problem. . . .

Subsequent epidemiological studies have led to results at times markedly different from those in the Midtown research. When they are more carefully examined, however, it is found that these studies are not strictly comparable. Actually the exact statistics, which depend heavily on the researcher's degree of psychoanalytic sophistication, are less important than the recognition that both the sociological and the psychiatric images of normality have to be drastically altered.

"NORMALITY" IN CANADA

Equally striking were the findings of the Stirling County study by Alexander Leighton and his associates, reported in three books: *My Name Is Legion* (1959), *People of Cove and Woodlot* (1960), and *The Character of Danger* (1963).

The Stirling County study was a project conducted by Cornell University in collaboration with the Department of Public Health of the Province of Nova Scotia. The pilot phase was conducted in Sterling County during the summers of 1948, 1949, and 1950. For the most part it was carried out by graduate students under the supervision of Leighton. Field operations began in 1951 and continued through 1956.

One of their main conclusions was that approximately two-thirds of the inhabitants of the county had suffered at some time during their lives from a psychiatric disorder, for the most part low-grade and chronic, according to the criteria of the APA Manual of Psychiatric Disorders.

These studies, as well as others along similar lines, have enormous implications for the relationship of the ego to society. Merton (1962) has suggested that the individual can resort to conformity, retreatism, ritualism, innovation, and rebelliousness; this classification deals primarily with action. In terms of the psyche he can also respond with anxiety, tension, guilt, shame, withdrawal, displacement, projection, and many other neurotic or psychotic mechanisms. In other words, the individual does internalize the values of his culture, but in doing so he develops a wide variety of neurotic and psychotic disorders. And the worse the social situation, the worse is his psychological response. Only a relatively small percentage of unusual individuals (about 20 percent in both studies) manage to grow up with a minimum of psychological conflicts, and it may well be that if these too had been examined more closely they would have displayed more conflict.

Again, it must be emphasized that the older notion of the "psychologically normal" man must be completely discarded. All cultures known to date have created people with emotional disabilities; the differences have only been ones of degree.

ALIENATION

ALIENATION AND CONFORMITY

In discussions of contemporary culture the concept of alienation has become a central concern. Many intellectuals from all fields have presented abundant evidence that modern life is a kind of endless crisis, that man lives estranged or alienated from his innermost core, and that this "sickness unto death," as Kierkegaard described it, must be cured or man will perish.

Although there is little doubt of the widespread malaise that grips contemporary man, the situation is still not so simple as it may appear. Alienation involves, to begin with, a sense of estrangement from the prevailing social system; the socially alienated is contrasted with the socially involved. But since the socially involved represent essentially an adjustment neurosis in any culture, the nature of alienation requires very careful examination.

Webster's Third New International Dictionary (1969) defines "alienate" as "to cause to be estranged: make unfriendly, hostile or indifferent where attachment formerly existed." In view of the numerous meanings attached to "alienation" by philosophers, psychologists, and others, the dictionary definition can be used as a convenient guide to the phenomena described.

The catastrophic series of shocks to which most men in modern times have been exposed would certainly be enough to make them unfriendly, indifferent, or hostile to the prevailing values of society, leading them to withdraw into a world of their own, which others then describe as alienated. However, this alienated withdrawal can be evaluated only in terms of its inner dynamics and the alternatives available to the individual.

Riesman (1961) has popularized the terms "other-directed" and "inner-directed." The other-directed man is the one for whom his contemporaries are the main source of direction, either those known to him or those with whom he is indirectly acquainted, through friends and through the mass media. This source is "internalized" in the sense that dependence on it for guidance in life is implanted early. The goals toward which the other-directed person strives shift with that guidance: it is only the process of striving itself and the process of paying close attention to the signals from others that remain unaltered throughout life. This mode of keeping in touch with others permits a close behavioral conformity, not through drill in behavior itself, as in the tradition-directed character, but rather through an exceptional sensitivity to the actions and wishes of others. This yearning for the approval of others covers up a deep inner sense of loneliness; hence the term "the lonely crowd." Riesman's conception is similar to what Fromm calls the "marketing personality," what Mills called the "fixer," and what Green called the "middle-class male child."

Nevertheless, while this description certainly has some truth to it, that truth is only partial. What Riesman is describing is more the superego that exists in every culture, forcing people to conform to mores they cannot even verbalize very often, whether they want to obey or not.

Many other aspects of the alienation of man have been described in this book. Looked at from the standpoint of the analytic ideal, man finds his life inadequate in a number of respects—lack of love, sexual frustration, lack of pleasure, excessive hatred, poor self-image, and so on.

On the other hand, the concept of alienation has been driven to preposterous extremes by some of its proponents. Thus Laing (1967) has been the prime advocate of the position that the schizophrenic somehow simply experiences the world in a different way, completely ignoring the terrible suffering that such individuals are going through. While it is true that some creative and brilliant people are misdiagnosed "schizophrenic" by poorly trained psychiatrists, it is equally true that most of the patients who fill the mental hospitals are neither brilliant nor creative, but simply unhappily and miserably infantile.

The psychoanalyst can also look upon himself as alienated from the society in which he lives. But he, and those who go along with his psychological attitudes, are in a position to change the society by changing the people in it, rather than withdrawing into some ivory tower sufficient unto themselves.

Nor is there much evidence that the alienation of modern man is such a peculiarly modern sickness, as many have tried to argue (Sorokin, 1941). It is in this respect that the presentation of history needs a sharp reversal, in line with the findings of modern psychology. Psychohistory would describe instead the myriad degrees of suffering, torture, madness, and murders that have afflicted man from time immemorial (Fine, 1971; Kaufmann, 1971). In a very real sense the world is less alienated than ever before, because for the first time in human history a large portion of mankind is seriously discussing the maladies that afflict society, and the remedies that may be able to cure them.

WORK

Although work and love are the two cornerstones of psycho-analytic philosophy, a comprehensive discussion of work is nowhere to be found in the psychoanalytic literature. Nor are any of the discussions in the psychological literature particularly illuminating. An adequate psychology-philosophy of work is urgently needed.

The idea that work can make men happy is a fairly novel one in human experience. Aristotle did not think so, nor did the Christians for many centuries look upon work as anything but an interference with service to God. In keeping with this ideology, the classical economists argued that man works only because he has to make money.

It is paradoxical that although Marx idealized labor to the point where all value comes from labor, and everything else is surplus value, he too had no really coherent theory of work. His whole philosophy is based on the notion of alienated labor, and the assumption that all labor before communism is reached is essentially alienated.

The most significant departure from classical theory was Max Weber's concept of a Protestant ethic, which has such a compelling quality that it has virtually become part of the language of every cultured man today (Weber, 1904). His central thesis is that modern capitalistic man is dominated by a special ethos, called the Protestant ethic, because it is far stronger in Protestant countries than in Catholic or non-Christian ones. This ethic emphasizes the virtues of industry, thrift, sobriety, work, and the accumulation of wealth, all of these having religious sanction. The *summum bonum* of this ethic is the earning of more and more money, combined with the strict avoidance of all spontaneous enjoyment of life.

A subsidiary confirmation of Weber's position is the work by McClelland on the achievement motive (1961). McClelland also emphasizes that what is basic to capitalism as well as to any other society that grows rapidly is a certain psychological frame of mind which stresses achievement, responsibility, enterprise, and growth. His thesis is that it is not profit per se that makes the businessman tick, but a strong desire for achievement in doing a good job. He has published a number of empirical studies that support this rather surprising thesis in a number of ways, currently and historically.

CONTEMPORARY VIEWS

Among economists the most prominent man who has attempted to unravel the psychology of work in contemporary society is John Kenneth Galbraith.

In his book *The New Industrial State* (1967) Galbraith offers a total revision of the psychological-economic bases of the system under which we are living. He makes free use of the findings of modern psychology and psychiatry.

He finds that there are four major motives that lead modern man to work: pecuniary compensation, compulsion, identification, and adaptation. These can motivate an individual either separately or in combination. The strength of any given motivation or of any motivating system will be measured by the effectiveness with which it aligns the individual with the goals of the organization.

HERZBERG AND THE HYGIENE-MOTIVATOR THEORY OF WORK SATISFACTION

Herzberg represents perhaps the best known and the most important of the empirical investigations of work satisfaction. His findings have been summarized in two books: *The Motivation to Work* (Herzberg et al., 1959) and *Work and the Nature of Man* (1966). The material here is taken primarily from the latter work.

Motivators and Dissatisfiers

On the basis of questionnaires submitted to two hundred engineers and accountants, Herzberg found that five factors, which he calls motivators, stand out as strong determiners of job satisfaction: achievement, recognition, work itself, responsibility, and advancement. The major factors that stand out as dissatisfiers are: company policy and administration, supervision, salary, interpersonal relations, and working conditions.

The motivators all seem to describe man's relationship to what he does: his job content, achievement on a test, recognition or task achievement, nature of the task, responsibility for the task, professional advancement, long-term growth in task capability.

The central theme for the dissatisfiers is that they describe man's relationship to the context or environment in which he does his job. Since these factors serve primarily to prevent job dissatisfaction while having little effect on positive job attitude, he calls them hygiene factors. This is an analogy to the medical term meaning preventive and environmental. Dissatisfying factors are not motivators since they are not effectively motivating the individual to superior performance and effort. The principal result of the analysis of the data was to suggest that the hygiene factors or maintenance of them must lead to job dissatisfaction because of a need to avoid unpleasantness; the motivators then lead to job satisfaction because of a need for growth or self-actualization.

MODERN CRITIQUE OF THE VALUE OF WORK

But paradoxically, yet not unexpectedly, the demand that work should be gratifying has brought about a searching reevaluation of the meaning of work to man, especially as the hold of religion and the Protestant ethic lessen. The most comprehensive examination of the American work experience is found in the report of a special task force to the Secretary of Health, Education and Welfare, published in book form with the title *Work in America* (1973).

The major study cited was based on a representative sample of 1,533 American workers at all occupational levels. It was undertaken by the Survey Research Center of the University of Michigan, with support from the Department of Labor.

Although a superficial Gallup poll question asking "Are you satisfied with your work?" evokes positive responses 80 to 90 percent of the time, any more sophisticated approach immediately reveals the deep dissatisfactions that affect the American worker. These can be grouped as follows:

1. *Blue-collar blues.* Work problems spill over from the factory into other activities of life; one frustrated assembly-line worker will displace his job-generated aggression on family, neighbors, and strangers, while a fellow worker comes home so fatigued from his day's work that all he can do is collapse and watch TV.

An earlier study of work alienation among 1,156 employed men revealed that the best independent predictors of work alienation are: (a) a work situation and hierarchical organization that provide little discretion in pace and schedule; (b) a career that has been blocked and chaotic; and (c) a stage in the life cycle that puts the squeeze on the worker (large numbers of dependent children and low amounts of savings).

2. *Worker mobility.* Many blue-collar workers do not believe that there is a great deal of opportunity to move up the ladder of success, and the lack of alternatives produces frustration. Further, manual work has increasingly become denigrated by the upper middle class.

3. *White-collar woes.* There is increasing evidence of managerial discontent. One out of three middle managers indicates some willingness to join a union, while a large percentage seek a change in middle life.

4. *The young worker challenging the work ethic.* A consistent attack on the Protestant ethic is found to be particularly strong among young people. Yankelovich (1972) found that in 1968, 69 percent expressed the belief that hard work will always pay off, while by 1971 this had fallen to 39 percent. Young managers reflect the passionate concern of youth in the 1970s for individuality, openness, humanism, concern, and change, and they are determined to be heard.

5. *The minority workers.* Minority workers and their families are serious casualties of the work system in our society. One out of three minority workers is unemployed, irregularly employed, or has given up looking for a job. Another third of minority workers do have jobs, full time, year round, but these are mainly laboring jobs and jobs in the service trades, which often pay less than a living wage.

6. *Women and work.* In addition to the fact that half of all women between eighteen and sixty-four are presently in the labor force, Department of Labor studies have shown that nine out of ten women will work outside the home at some time in their lives. Because of the widespread dissatisfaction with the kinds of jobs that women have

traditionally held, women can be expected to speak out ever more forcefully on the quality of working life.

7. *Older workers and retirement.* In 1900, two-thirds of American men who were sixty-five years old and older were working. By 1971, the figure had dropped to one-fourth, with a smaller proportion on a year-round, full-time basis. Most of the members of this age group today are expected to retire. The problem that has arisen is the inadequacy of pension plans.

8. *Work and health.* A surprisingly positive correlation exists between work and satisfaction and physical and mental health. In one fifteen-year study of aging (Palmare, 1969), the strongest predictor of longevity was work satisfaction.

WORK AND THE ROLES OF MAN

Man can be said to have three roles: a work role, a love role, and a play role. If the totality of anyone's life is to be grasped, his functioning in all three of these roles must be investigated.

The *work role* is the one in which modern man has achieved most success. He can work and achieve beyond the wildest dreams of man even a hundred years ago. But he does so at a price.

This price has varied at different times in the past centuries. At present, work is still maintained by a denigration of the love role and the play role. The correction of these imbalances is one task of the next few generations. In this sense the constant diminution of the work week, the increasing use of leisure time (even avocational counselors now exist in large number), and the steady freeing of the sex life are all part of one whole, the creation of a more satisfied type of person.

In practice there are varying relationships among the three roles. The ideal of a harmonious balance is rarely found. More often than not, work achievement is reached at the expense of a miserable love life and an absence of play. Various other combinations are possible. Only one thing is certain: no work achievement, no matter how great, affords the individual real happiness if there is an imbalance among the three roles.

FREE WILL AND ACTION

The problem of freedom of the will is one of the historically insoluble problems of philosophy. Without offering a complete solution, psychoanalysis is in a position to make a considerable contribution, and to narrow the problem considerably. Compulsive behavior is understandable in terms of its dependency on unconscious motives; action and desire become less compulsive as the motives are brought to consciousness. Free will is thus possible only in a state of full consciousness. Thus here too consciousness becomes one of the signposts of mental health.

Freedom of action represents a complex problem. Parsons and Shils (1951) have attempted to rewrite sociology as a science of action. Schafer (1973) has recently announced his intention of rewriting psychoanalysis in terms of a theory of action. Apart from other problems involved, the prime difficulty lies in distinguishing between acting out and free action; as with free will, the latter depends on full consciousness. To determine when an action is dictated by conscious and when by unconscious motives is obviously extraordinarily difficult, in most cases calling for extensive inference from available data. This fact poses a major problem for all the social sciences.

CHAPTER 16

Psychiatric Symptomatology

Every mental health professional knows that the current situation in psychiatry, as in all the mental health fields, is utterly chaotic. To understand this chaos it is necessary to know the history of psychiatry. What is seen nowadays is the result of a crazy patchwork of ill-assorted and unrelated developments. While psychiatry has a long past, it has a short history. Kraepelin and Freud were contemporaries; virtually all of psychiatry was developed at the same time as psychoanalysis. Kraepelin's definitive edition of his textbook, which provided the groundwork for what has since been known as Kraepelinian or organic psychiatry, was published in 1899. Freud's first major paper was "The Neuro-psychoses of Defense," published in 1894. Psychiatry and psychology, both essentially products of the twentieth century, developed along two competing lines; their intersection, in this country, is primarily a historical accident.

Webster's Third New International Dictionary defines psychiatry as "a branch of medicine that deals with the science and practice of treating mental, emotional and behavioral disorders especially as originating in endogenous causes or resulting from faulty interpersonal relationships." This is a rather peculiar definition. It lumps together mental, emotional, and behavioral disorders, not even trying to distinguish among them. Why it stresses endogenous causes is not clear. And above all it avoids the major historical question: Why should medicine be called upon to handle faulty interpersonal relationships? This would seem to be rather the domain of religion or philosophy or ethics or social regulation, not of organic medicine as such.

While textbooks provide details on when various diagnostic entities were first described, they usually fail to state that the history of psychiatry prior to the twentieth century is a history of colossal error. It is also a history of extraordinary cruelty. Kraepelin himself, in *One Hundred Years of Psychiatry* (1917), described what preceded him in these terms:

> The broad outlines of the practice of psychiatry as it existed a century ago have been revealed by our cursory survey: negligent and brutal treatment of the insane; improper living conditions and inadequate medical care; beclouded and false notions concerning the nature and cause of insanity; senseless, haphazard and at times harmful therapeutic measures which aggravated the plight of those afflicted by mental illness.

But if the treatment of the mentally ill was barbarous and cruel before Kraepelin, under the aegis of his system, the schizophrenic was shocked, injected almost to death, castrated, lobotomized; had all his teeth extracted and his intestines removed; bound hand and foot, beaten by careless attendants, and largely neglected in filthy, poorly kept "mental hospitals," which are now being systematically dismantled.

SOMATIC FACTORS

Medicine entered into the study and treatment of mental and emotional disturbance on the hypothesis that these were illnesses, like the physical ones, that could be caused organically, and treated by somatic and pharmacological means. The discovery of the syphilitic origin of general paresis and the spike potential in epilepsy lent impetus to the search for the "schizobacillus" and related organisms. In spite of extensive research, the field is full of speculation with little or no factual basis.

Beginning with the 1950s the advent of the phenothiazines and other tranquilizers led to a new era of hopefulness in psychiatry about the possibilities of somatic treatment, and eventual discovery of somatic etiology. Since then psychiatrists have been trained in a mixture of somatic and psychological therapies, adopting generally an eclectic position, somewhere between the psychological assumptions of psychoanalysis and the organic ones of Kraepelinian psychiatry. A full evaluation of this question is beyond the scope of this book, but the following comments are pertinent.

Despite an enormous expenditure of time and energy on research, the organic basis for schizophrenia, including the hereditary factor, remains a purely speculative hypothesis.

As of the latest review (Lidz, 1973), again nothing definitive has been demonstrated. No doubt some of the patients called schizophrenic have some organic pathology, but they would appear to be a relative minority. As of 1968, Bellak ventured the guess that in 50 percent of schizophrenic patients purely psychogenic factors play the primary role in etiology (Bellak and Loeb, 1968, p. 779). Yet even in those in whom the major etiological factors are organic, sociopsychological factors play an important function in determining the course and ultimate outcome of the illness.

The same considerations apply *a fortiori* to all the diagnostic entities listed in the standard DSM (Diagnostic and Statistical Manual, 1968) issued by the American Psychiatric Association; while knowledge of physiological factors has increased enormously, so far as can be seen psychosocial factors play the major role in all areas of psychiatric disturbance, and where physiological factors can be implicated, it should be done only on the basis of precise and ascertainable clinical knowledge.

With regard to treatment, even though pharmacological therapy has become routine in all psychiatric practice, its theoretical rationale is at best shaky, while even its practical effectiveness is open to increasing question by a number of clinicians (Cancro, Fox, and Shapiro, 1974). Beginning in the early 1960s the secular trend toward steadily increasing population in the mental hospital has been reversed. Instead, the patients have been shifted to community mental health centers, following the passage of an act financing such centers by the Kennedy administration. The population of the mental hospitals has indeed exhibited a dramatic drop, but the qualitative meaning of this wholesale discharge process is far from clear. Many have argued that it involves little more than a shift of helpless individuals from one environment to another, without any real inner change, regardless of whether tranquilizers are employed on a large scale or not. And the Nader group's recent report on the community mental health centers (Chu and Trotter, 1974) castigates contemporary psychiatric practices mercilessly.

Forward-looking psychiatrists freely admit the need for an extensive reform of their field. In a recent evaluation Milton Greenblatt, former Commissioner of Mental Hygiene of Massachusetts, writes (1964, pp. 1200-1201):

> Although it is an indelible blot on the escutcheon, we must admit poverty and deprivation still prevail in most of the large mental institutions in the United States. Poverty is not new in America, but the mentally ill and the mentally retarded are poor many times over. They come from poor backgrounds, they are poor in mental and often physical health, we treat them in poverty-stricken institutions, and then we return them to their poverty-ridden surroundings—often, inevitably, to begin the cycle again.

THE EXPANSION OF PSYCHIATRY
THROUGH PSYCHOANALYSIS

The expansion of psychiatry into philosophy, society, religion, history, and other areas of the social sciences is due entirely to its incorporation of psychoanalysis; Kraepelin had no use for these auxiliary sciences, nor could he conceivably have fitted them into his rigid system, based on "hereditary degeneration" and brain pathology. Modern psychiatry has become a fusion of the organic approach, derived from Kraepelin, and the psychological, derived from Freud. The paradox is that the psychiatrist, who a hundred years ago was almost at the bottom of the medical ladder, just a notch above the ship's doctor, and has now become one of the most respected and highly honored members of the medical profession, owes his prestige largely to the fact that he was willing to study psychology. Academic psychology, by contrast, remained distant from human concerns, and was left behind to putter about in its experimental ivory towers (Fine, 1970).

PSYCHIATRY AS A FORM OF PSYCHOHISTORY

The broad outcome of psychoanalytic research in the present century is that mental illness represents an inability to love, resulting in excessive hatred. Organic psychiatry was for a long time, and still is, oblivious of the significance of hatred. Sociologically, the listings of diagnoses ("demons") and the search for organic causes covered up the deep-seated damage that hatreds do to the individual and to the social order. It is this that makes the whole history of psychiatry before psychoanalysis one gigantic blunder.

The concept of illness is inseparable from the image of health. There is every reason to believe that mankind has always existed in a state of severe emotional disturbance. Hence the "insane" in any century represent the maladjustment neurosis of that time, while the "sane" represent the adjustment neurosis. There can be little doubt that from the vantage point of the analytic ideal the maladjusted have many times been closer to mental health than the adjusted. Even with our advanced level of sophistication, in many cases this is true today as well.

Consider, for example, the prostitution of psychiatry in the ante bellum South, with its "diagnoses" of "dysaesthesia Aethiopis" and "drapetomania," which Szasz (1971) has unearthed. Or the prostitution of psychiatry in the contemporary Soviet Union, where there seems to be a systematic procedure of hounding political dissenters into psychiatric hospitals (Medvedev, 1971). While such excesses are rarely seen in the United States today, there are undoubtedly many psychiatrists who impose their personal values on the people whom they treat, rationalizing these values under the name of diagnoses. Thus it has become quite common to call a patient schizophrenic if he does something the psychiatrist thinks is wrong. Here too political dissenters may be considered mentally ill, although their treatment is not nearly so harsh as in the USSR.

Literally the term "psychiatrist" means physician of the mind. It was not until the French Revolution that medically trained physicians began to take over the treatment of the insane. They took it over from the clergy, who had tortured and murdered the disturbed, especially unhappy women, for several centuries. Physicians at that time had no clue to what made people so bizarre, but they could and did give the patient more humane treatment than he had ever received before. It is somewhat ironic that today many feel that brutal treatment is administered by physicians, while kindness is shown by the clergy. Hence it is not surprising that the pendulum is swinging the other way, and that the mentally disturbed are turning away from psychiatry to the social disciplines, including religion.

"ILLNESS" AS DISTANCE FROM THE ANALYTIC IDEAL

From a psychological point of view it is possible to define the degree of emotional disturbance as the distance from the analytic ideal. This distance can vary for the different components of the ideal; it can be great in some, slight in others. In more technical language Freud made this point with his remark that the ego of the normal individual can vary from normal to psychotic, depending on the area investigated (1937, p. 235). Such a position permits the evaluation of other cultures, as well as our own, without calling normal everything that is done daily.

Dynamic psychiatry (psychoanalysis) today places the emphasis on the character structure (ego) rather than on the symptom. No symptom can be understood without reference to the context.

EGO FUNCTIONS PROFILE
(METAPSYCHOLOGICAL ASSESSMENT)

Because of the many defects inherent in the current diagnostic system, dynamically oriented clinicians have increasingly moved to a metapsychological assessment, rather than one global description. The most recent advance in this approach is the ego functions profile of Bellak (Bellak, Hurvich, and Gediman, 1973). This profile enumerates twelve ego functions: reality testing, judgment, sense of reality of the world and of the self, regulation and control of drives, affects and impulses, object relations, thought processes, adaptive regression in the service of the ego, defensive functioning, stimulus barrier, autonomous functioning, synthetic-integrative functioning, and mastery-competence.

Scoring of the various ego functions leads to a profile on which a patient can be high in some areas, low in others. Simple summations of the person's state are misleading: everything has to be considered. In this way Bellak has put into statistically manipulatable form the dynamic observations derived from psychoanalytic research. Again it must be emphasized that this in no way excludes any organic information.

There is no good substitute for the complex metapsychological assessment profile. A number of other assessment profiles can be found in the literature. All of these follow the same essential principle of describing as fully as possible all aspects of the personality in dynamic terms.

INSANITY AND THE SOCIAL STRUCTURE

In a most significant book George Rosen (1968) has gathered together much evidence concerning the relationship between insanity and the social structure in various historical epochs. Saul, the first king of the Jews (reigned 1020-1000 B.C.), was described as mad by the biblical writers. He developed a hatred of David, who at first was a favorite who could charm away Saul's spells with his music. Eventually Saul was killed in a battle to exterminate David. Samuel the Prophet had earlier ordered Saul in the name of the Lord to extirpate the people of Amalek, to put to the sword "both man and woman, infant and suckling, ox and sheep, camel and ass." When Saul disobeyed this prophetic injunction he was allegedly driven mad in retaliation.

Throughout history the madman has been seen as either a genius or a devil. In our contemporary society, he has been the scapegoat for a century or more. The origins of this attitude have been traced by Michel Foucault (1965). He shows how the mental asylum gradually replaced the hospitals for lepers, situated at the outskirts of the city, when leprosy suddenly and mysteriously disappeared as a major scourge. Once the asylums were set up, people began to fear that they too were crazy and would have to be confined like the poor inmates. We know today that the schizophrenic individual is the scapegoat of his family (cf. Lidz, 1973; Ackerman, 1958); the family scapegoat has thus also served for several hundred years as society's scapegoat. In this process obviously the original paranoid constellation is doubly reinforced by social actions inimical to the individual. Even the humanitarian ideals of the French Revolution, which led Pinel to free the mentally ill from their chains, ran up against this horrible fear, and the populace strenuously objected to Pinel's leniency. Much the same has occurred in our own day. The Cummings (1957) have documented their inability to convince the residents of a small Canadian community of the harmlessness of mental illness, while many have repeatedly objected to the installation of clinics for released mental patients, drug addicts, and alcoholics in their neighborhoods.

It should not be supposed that these historical observations of the prevalence of mental illness are irrelevant to what is going on today. The extraordinary conflagration of World War II, which probably killed more people than all previous wars in history, was dominated by two individuals, Hitler and Stalin, who were no less mad than many of the denizens of mental hospitals. The major difference was that Hitler and Stalin could direct their mad hatreds outward, while the average schizophrenic directs them against himself.

Analytic theory enters a sobering caution about the meaning of these historical events. For it is known that the leader of any group embodies the superego and the ideals of that group; so that if the leader is mad, the group is not far off. It is this that has led to the increasing realization that the proper psychological evaluation of men is a prime necessity in all societies. Unfortunately all too often "establishment" psychiatry has served chiefly as a social rationalization to avoid looking at the deep-seated disturbances in the ruling groups.

PSYCHOTHERAPY, PSYCHIATRY, AND SOCIAL REFORM

The relationship of the social structure to psychiatric disturbance is not a superficial or insignificant one; it cuts through to the very heart of the problem. The gross disturbances in any period are exaggerations of those that are found in all people at that time; where one ends and the other begins is highly arbitrary. The entire corpus of knowledge that we call psychology and psychiatry today leads to the momentous conclusion that it is essential to reorganize the total social structure along the lines of the analytic ideal. Hence psychotherapy is inherently a means of social reform.

Every society tells its members, explicitly or implicitly, that if they observe the ethos of the community they will be happy. Any unhappiness, the general assumption holds, must come from extra-social sources—magic, sorcery, agitators, brain pathology, and the like. As has been seen, the trouble with this assumption is that it is simply untrue. For the most part unhappiness that does not conflict with social custom too sharply has simply been ignored.

Modern psychosocial research has solidly established the fact that each society creates certain kinds of unhappiness which it considers perfectly normal. We can speak in every case of an adjustment neurosis and of a maladjustment neurosis. Only the latter has been given much consideration historically; for an understanding of the former we must turn to the insights of psychotherapy. What we are talking about here is the adjustment neurosis of our own society.

Social reformers have generally been interested in institutions rather than people. Get rid of private property, the Marxists argued, and you will have done away with hostility. History has not borne them out. Unionize the workers, give them good living conditions, the liberal labor movement held, and they will be happy. The facts are otherwise.

This should not be construed as any argument against social reform. Quite the contrary. The institutions of society should be altered in many ways, but it is important to realize what will be accomplished by such institutional change and what will not. The inner discontent of man is not materially affected by such outer changes; that can be attacked only internally.

Religious thinkers have generally urged men to forget the world and find the kingdom of heaven within: "Render unto Caesar the things that are Caesar's, and to God the things that are God's" was the solution in the early days of Christianity. There are two difficulties with this approach. First, it is impossible. Religious freedom can exist only within a certain social order, and religion cannot forget the social order. The Romans tolerated Christianity, but the Christians themselves, when they became the caesars, did not tolerate any form other than their own versions, often pretty narrowly defined. And second, the inner happiness that religion offers is either illusory or not the kind that appeals to the sophisticated man of today (or other days, for that matter). It is too opposed to indestructible human needs, such as sexuality or the need for communication. It rests upon guilt imposed by authority, rather than self-actualization.

If there is a real external problem, the patient in psychotherapy must learn how to handle it. On a larger scale, if there are oppressive social conditions, men must feel strong enough to change them, sometimes, if necessary, by force. Not turning the other cheek, but the normal use of aggression is what is required.

SOCIAL REFORM AND INNER CHANGE

But again following the analogy of individual psychotherapy, the social change alone does not bring happiness; it merely paves the way for it. It must be followed up by inner change if happiness is the goal.

As an example, take the case of nationalism. Freedom from external oppression has always been a cry that could rally men to the flag. Yet once freedom is achieved, as it has been over and over again, the same problems recur.

On the other hand, psychotherapy differs from religion in that its philosophy of living is closer to man's essential nature. A further difference lies in the recognition of the human need for communication, and the provision of adequate means for satisfying this need (group therapy, group discussions under trained leaders).

Paradoxically, psychotherapeutic social reform thus steers a middle road between traditional external change of the social institutions and traditional religious inner transformation. Based on a scientific understanding of human nature, it seeks to build a better world by a persistent gradual change of the present one. Its major contribution lies in the recognition that there are many inner conflicts that can be changed only psychotherapeutically.

The other parts of the psychotherapeutic philosophy have already been discussed at sufficient length—pleasure, sex, feelings, promotion of love, restriction of hatred, family role, identity, work, and creativity. None of these is novel in the history of man; what is novel is their unification into a cohesive way of living.

Other philosophies, both past and present, have overemphasized one aspect of living at the cost of others. Thus pure hedonism does often lead to excesses that are harmful; e.g., it has frequently led to a great deal of violence. The advocacy of feeling by the romantics was all too frequently coupled with intense suffering, since that is a feeling too. On the other hand, the bourgeois image of the family has created people who look like characters in Grant Wood's pictures—lifeless, without zest, spontaneity, or feeling.

A PSYCHOTHERAPEUTIC VISION OF HAPPINESS

What the psychotherapeutic philosophy stresses is balance. To some extent a person must participate in each aspect of the ideal to have a happy life. No doubt the different ingredients will vary from person to person, but it is well to remember our clinical experience that extremes in any direction produce much misery.

It may be objected that a psychotherapeutic vision of human happiness is completely unrealistic at the present juncture. And yet a vision, even if it cannot be realized in the immediate future, serves a constructive purpose. It is better to light a candle than to curse the darkness. History has played a curious trick on mankind in that physics and psychology both have reached a stage of world-shaking maturity at the same time. Just when man discovered the means by which he could effect his own destruction, he was also in the process of perfecting techniques for securing his salvation.

The physicists have responded to the challenge by forming political action committees. Although as scientists we are always humble about the vastness of our ignorance, we should also be cognizant of the magnitude of our achievements. Psychology, in spite of all its limitations, has come along far enough to offer a positive program for happiness.

CHAPTER 17

Summary and Conclusions

This book has proposed a systematic approach to psychology along psychoanalytic lines. Such an approach is based on the concept of the analytic ideal, which assumes that man finds his greatest degree of happiness if he can love, have pleasure, enjoy sex, have feeling yet be guided by reason, play a role in a family and in a wider social structure, have a sense of identity, communicate, be creative, work, and be free from psychiatric symptomatology. For each of these components of the analytic ideal, psychological considerations mesh with philosophical ones into a rounded theory.

Methodologically, the major pathways to knowledge rely on integration of material from many different sources. At the present time, by and large observation proves to be more important than experiment. Most important of all is the conceptual framework offered by psychoanalysis, which provides a home for the data and suggests meaningful directions in which research should move.

With regard to psychoanalysis, the stress has been on the core of psychodynamic understanding beginning with Freud, but going well beyond him in virtually all areas. Actually review of the material shows that the common division into "schools" has arisen because of deep-seated personal rivalries, and not because it is inherent in the field. The attempt has consistently been made to integrate all meaningful data into one comprehensive theory, regardless of where the

171

data come from. When that is done it becomes plain that contributions to dynamic psychology have come from many different persons, and that the "schools" to which they claim to belong have little relevance. Psychoanalytic psychology should be handled like all other sciences, in terms of issues rather than persons.

With regard to psychology, the expansion into dynamic clinical fields has necessarily brought in all the facts and theories of psychoanalysis. Here the experimental approach has added so little that the absolute insistence that it is the *sine qua non* of science must be rejected. In the classical areas of psychology, the study of the cognitive functions, considerable revision is required to make the results applicable to the functioning human being. The framework of the ego, with its division into defensive and autonomous aspects, and their interactions, has been suggested as one that offers the most fruitful avenue available for the study of these problems.

In the other social sciences, the elaboration of a systematic approach would have taken us too far, so that these areas have only been touched upon in the most cursory manner. In principle, however, they can be handled in the same way, via the relative contributions of the defensive and autonomous ego. In all of them reformulations in psychological terms are going on all the time on the current scene; e.g., psychohistory, or the most recent applications to law (Slovenko, 1973).

The twentieth has been called the century of psychology because for the first time in human history a scientific road to happiness has become possible. In order to do that many of the sources of unhappiness institutionalized in all countries on the current scene have to be brought to light. The consequent criticism of the social order lends psychology much of its controversial character. While much remains to be done, enough has already been accomplished to make reasonable suggestions both for the expansion of knowledge and the attainment of greater happiness for mankind.

BIBLIOGRAPHY

Abbreviations used:

IJP—*International Journal of Psychoanalysis*
JAPA—*Journal of the American Psychoanalytic Association*
PQ—*Psychoanalytic Quarterly*
PSC—*Psychoanalytic Study of the Child*
PSM—*Psychosomatic Medicine*

Abend, S. M. 1954. Problems of Identity. *PQ* 43:606-37.
Abraham, K. 1953. *Selected Papers on Psychoanalysis*. New York Basic Books.
———. 1925. *Clinical Papers and Essays on Psychoanalysis*. New York: Basic Books.
Abrahamsen, D. 1973. *The Murdering Mind*. New York: Harper & Row.
Ackerman, N. 1958. *The Psychodynamics of Family Life*. New York: Basic Books.
Adorno, T. W.; Frankel-Brunswick, E.; Levinson, D.; and Sanford, B. 1950. *The Authoritarian Personality*. New York: Harper & Row.
Ahlstrom, W., and Havinghurst, R. 1971. *400 Losers*. San Francisco: Jossey-Bass.
Aichhorn, A. 1935. *Wayward Youth*. New York: Viking Press.
Alexander, F. 1923. The Castration Complex in the Formation of Character. In *The Scope of Psychoanalysis: Selected Papers of Franz Alexander*. New York: Basic Books, 1961.
Allen, V., ed. 1970. *Psychological Factors in Poverty*. Chicago: Markham.
Allport, G. W., and Postman, L. 1947. *The Psychology of Rumor*. New York: Holt, Rinehart & Winston.
Almond, R. 1974. *The Healing Community*. New York: Jason Aronson.
Andreski, S. 1972. *Social Sciences as Sorcery*. New York: St. Martin's Press.
Applegarth, A. 1971. Comments on Aspects of the Theory of Psychic Energy. *JAPA* 19:379-416.
Arlow, J. A. 1973. Perspectives on Aggression in Human Adaptation. *PQ* 42:178-84.
———, and Brenner, C. 1964. *Psychoanalytic Concepts and the Structural Theory*. New York: International Universities Press.
Aserinsky, E., and Kleitman, N. 1953. Regularly Occurring Periods of Eye Motility, and Concomitant Phenomena During Sleep. *Science* 118:273-74.
Baittle, B., and Offer, D. 1971. On the Nature of Male Adolescent Rebellion. In

Adolescent Psychiatry, ed. S. Feinstein, J. Giovacchini, and A. Miller, pp. 139-60. New York: Basic Books.

Bakan, D. 1967. *On Method.* San Francisco: Jossey-Bass.

Balint, M. 1953. *Primary Love and Psychoanalytic Technique.* New York: Liveright.

Bandura, A. 1973. *Aggression.* Englewood Cliffs, N.J.: Prentice-Hall.

Barber, T., et al., eds. 1971. *Biofeedback and Self-Control.* Chicago: Aldine-Atherton.

Bartell, G. 1971. *Group Sex.* New York: New American Library.

Bartlett, F. 1932. *Remembering.* Cambridge: Cambridge University Press.

Bateson, G.; Jackson, D.; Haley, J.; and Weakland, J. 1956. Toward a Theory of Schizophrenia. *Behav. Sci.* 1:251-64.

Bellak, L. 1961. Free Association. *IJP* 42:9-20.

————, Hurvich, M., and Gediman, H. 1973. *Ego Functions in Schizophrenics, Neurotics, and Normals.* New York: Wiley.

————, and Loeb, L. 1968. *The Schizophrenic Syndrome.* New York: Grune & Stratton.

Benedek, T. 1973. *Psychoanalytic Investigations.* New York: Quadrangle Books.

Benedict, R. 1934. *Patterns of Culture.* Boston: Houghton Mifflin.

Beres, D. 1960. The Psychoanalytic Psychology of Imagination. *JAPA* 8:252-69.

Berg, I. A. 1967. *Response Set in Personality Assessment.* Chicago: Aldine.

Berkman, T. 1972. *To Seize the Passing Dream: A Novel of Whistler, His Women and His World.* New York: Doubleday.

Berkowitz, L., ed. 1969. *The Roots of Aggression.* New York: Atherton.

Bieber, I., et al. 1962. *Homosexuality.* New York: Basic Books.

Bion, W. R. 1959. *Experiences in Groups.* New York: Basic Books.

Birch, H., ed. 1964. *Brain Damage in Children.* Baltimore: Williams & Wilkins.

Birdwhistle, R. 1970. *Kinesis and Context.* Philadelphia: University of Pennsylvania Press.

Blau, P. M., and Duncan, O. 1967. *The American Occupational Structure.* New York: Wiley.

Blos, P. 1962. *On Adolescence.* New York: Free Press.

Boas, F. 1905. The History of Anthropology. *Science* 20:513-24.

Bordin, E. S. 1966. Personality and Free Association. *J. Consult. Psychol.* 30: 30-38.

Bott, E. 1957. *Family and Social Network.* London: Tavistock, 1971.

Bourne, G., and Dominowsky, R. L. 1972. Thinking. In *Annual Reviews in Psychology* 23:105-30.

Bowlby, J. 1969. *Attachment,* vol. 1. New York: Basic Books.

————. 1973. *Attachment and Loss, vol. 2: Separation.* New York: Basic Books.

Boyer, L. B. 1961. Notes on the Personality Structure of a North American Indian Shaman. *J. of Hillside Hosp.* 10:14-33.

————, and Giovacchini, P. L. 1967. *Psychoanalytic Treatment of Characterological and Schizophrenic Disorders.* New York: Jason Aronson.

Brenman, M., and Gill, M. M. 1961. *Hypnosis and Related States.* New York: International Universities Press.

Brenner, C. 1971. Aggression. *IJP* 52:143-48.

————. 1972. *An Elementary Textbook of Psychoanalysis.* New York: International Universities Press.

Brierley, M. 1951. *Trends in Psychoanalysis.* London: Hogarth Press.

Brill, H. 1967. Nosology. In *Comprehensive Textbook of Psychiatry,* ed. A. Freedman and H. Kaplan, pp. 581-89. Baltimore: Williams & Wilkins.

Brody, S. 1956. *Patterns of Mothering.* New York: International Universities Press.

———. 1964. *Passivity.* New York: International Universities Press.

———, and Axelrad, S. 1970. *Anxiety and Ego Formation in Infancy.* New York: International Universities Press.

Bromberg, N. 1959. Stimulus-Response Cycle and Masochistic Ego. *JAPA* 7:225-49.

Brown, J. 1969. Female Initiation Rites: A Review of the Current Literature. In *Issues in Adolescent Psychology,* ed. D. Rogers, pp. 74-87. New York: Appleton-Century-Crofts.

Bruch, H. 1973. *Eating Disorders.* New York: Basic Books.

Burnham, D. L.; Gladstone, A. I.; and Gibson, R. W. 1969. *Schizophrenia and the Need-Fear Dilemma.* New York: International Universities Press.

Burrows, E. G. 1963. *Flower in My Ear.* Seattle: University of Washington Press.

Burton, R. V., and Whiting, W. 1969. The Absent Father and Cross-Sex Identity. In *Issues in Adolescent Psychology,* ed. D. Rogers, pp. 62-64. New York: Appleton-Century-Crofts.

Butcher, J. N., ed. 1972. *Objective Personality Assessment.* New York: Academic Press.

Bychowski, G. 1958. The Struggle Against the Introjects. *IJP* 39:182-87.

Campbell, J. 1949. *The Hero with a Thousand Faces.* New York: Meridian Books, 1956.

Cancro, R.; Fox, N.; and Shapiro, L. 1974. *Strategic Intervention in Schizophrenia.* New York: Behavioral Publications.

Cannon, W. B. 1932. *The Wisdom of the Body.* New York: Norton, 1963.

Cappellanus, A. 1180. *The Art of Courtly Love.* New York: Norton, 1969.

Center for Integrative Education. 1972. *Main Currents in Modern Thought,* vol. 29, no. 1. New Rochelle, N.Y.

Chein, I.; Gerard, D.; Lee, R.; and Rosenfeld, E. 1964. *The Road to H.* New York: Basic Books.

Chinoy, E. 1955. *Automobile Workers and the American Dream.* New York: Random House.

Chomsky, N. 1968. *Language and Mind.* New York: Harcourt, Brace & World.

Choun, S. 1972. *Human Aging.* Baltimore: Penguin Books.

Chu, F. D., and Trotter, S. 1974. *The Madness Establishment.* New York: Grossman.

Cofer, C., and Appley, M. 1964. *Motivation: Theory and Research.* New York: Wiley.

Cohen, Y. 1966. *The Transition from Childhood to Adolescence.* Chicago: Aldine.

Coleman, J. R., et al. 1966. *Equality of Educational Opportunity.* Washington, D.C.: U.S. Department of Health, Education, and Welfare.

Compton, A. 1972. A Study of the Psychoanalytic Theory of Anxiety. *JAPA* 20:3-44.

Cronbach, L. J. 1957. The Two Disciplines of Scientific Psychology. *Amer. Psychologist,* 12:671-84.

Cuber, J., and Harroff, P. 1965. *The Significant Americans.* New York: Appleton-Century-Crofts.

Cumming, E., and Cumming, J. 1957. *Closed Ranks.* Cambridge: Harvard University Press.

Danielsson, B. 1956. *Love in the South Seas.* New York: Reynal.

Davidson, S. 1961. School Phobia as a Manifestation of Family Disturbance: Its Structure and Treatment. *J. Child Psychol. Psychiat.* 1:270-87.

Davis, D. B. 1966. *The Problem of Slavery in Western Culture.* Ithaca: Cornell University Press.

Dawson, J. 1964. Urbanization and Mental Health in a West African Community. In *Magic, Faith, and Healing,* ed. A. Kiev. New York: Free Press.

De George, R. T. 1966. *Patterns of Soviet Thought.* Ann Arbor: University of Michigan Press.

De Mause, L. 1974. *The History of Childhood.* New York: Psychohistory Press.

Dember, W. N. 1960. *Psychology of Perception.* New York: Holt, Rinehart & Winston.

Deutsch, H. 1945. *The Psychology of Women, 2* vols. New York: Grune & Stratton.

De Vos, G., and Hippler, A. A. 1969. Cultural Psychology: Comparative Studies of Human Behavior. In *Handbook of Social Psychology,* ed. G. Lindzey and E. Aronson, pp. 323-417. Reading, Mass.: Addison-Wesley.

Diamond, S. 1974. *In Search of the Primitive.* New Brunswick, N.J.: Transaction Books.

Dillard, J. L. 1972. *Black English.* New York: Random House.,

Dollard, J., and Miller, N. 1939. *Frustration and Aggression.* New Haven: Yale University Press.

Domhoff, G. W. 1967. *Who Rules America?* Englewood Cliffs, N.J.: Prentice-Hall.

Douglas, M. 1970. *Natural Symbols.* New York: Random House.

Dunbar, F. 1935. *Emotions and Bodily Changes.* New York: Columbia University Press.

Duncan, C. P.; Sechrest, L.; and Melton, A. 1972. *Human Memory.* New York: Appleton-Century-Crofts.

Duncan, O.; Featherman, D.; and Duncan, B. 1972. *Socioeconomic Background and Achievement.* New York: Seminar Press.

Eaton, J. W., and Weil, R. J. 1955. The Mental Health of the Hutterites. In *Culture and Mental Disorders,* ed. M. Opler. New York: Free Press.

Eck, M. 1970. *Lies and Truth.* New York: Macmillan.

Egbert, D. 1970. *Social Radicalism and the Arts.* New York: Knopf.

Eisenberg, L. 1957. The Fathers of Autistic Children. *Amer. J. Orthopsych.* 27: 715-24.

Eisenstadt, S. N. 1969. Archetypal Patterns of Youth. In *Issues in Adolescent Psychology,* ed. D. Rogers, pp. 565-75. New York: Appleton-Century-Crofts.

Ekstein, R., and Motto, R. L. 1973. *From Learning for Love to Love of Learning.* New York: Brunner/Mazel.

Ellenberger, H. F. 1970. *The Discovery of the Unconscious.* New York: Basic Books.

Erikson, E. 1950. *Childhood and Society.* New York: Norton.

―――. 1968. *Identity, Youth, and Crisis.* New York: Norton.

Fairfield, R. 1972. *Communes USA.* Baltimore: Penguin Books.

Federn, P. 1952. *Ego Psychology and the Psychoses.* New York: Basic Books.

Feinsilver, D. 1971. Communication in Families of Schizophrenic Patients. In *The Schizophrenic Syndrome: An Annual Review,* ed. R. Cancro, 1:257-67. New York: Brunner/Mazel.

Fenichel, O. 1945. *The Psychoanalytic Theory of Neurosis.* New York: Norton.

Feuer, L. 1969. *The Conflict of Generations.* New York: Basic Books.

Fine, R. 1958-1959. The Logic of Psychology. *Psychoanalysis and the Psychoanalytic Review* 45:15-41.

―――. 1960-1961. The Measurement Problem in Psychology. *Psychoanalysis and the Psychoanalytic Review.*

―――. 1967. *The Psychology of the Chess Player.* New York: Dover.

―――. 1969. On the Nature of Scientific Method in Psychology. *Psychological Reports* 24:519-40.

―――. 1970. Psychoanalysis, Psychology, and Psychotherapy. *Psychotherapy: Theory, Research, and Practice,* 7 (no. 2): 120-24.

―――. 1971. *The Healing of the Mind.* New York: McKay.

―――. 1972. The Age of Awareness. *Psychoanalytic Review* 59:55-71.

————. 1973a. A Critical Examination of the Concept of Acting Out. In *Acting Out: The Neurosis of Our Times*, ed. G. Goldman and D. Milman, pp. 5-20. Springfield, Ill.: Charles C Thomas.

————. 1973b. *The Development of Freud's Thought*. New York: Jason Aronson.

Fisher, C. 1957. A Study of the Preliminary Stages of the Construction of Dreams and Images. *JAPA* 5:5-60.

————. 1965. Psychoanalytic Implications of Recent Research on Sleep and Dreaming. *JAPA* 13:197-303.

———— et al. 1970. A Psychophysiological Study of Nightmares. *JAPA* 18:747-82.

Fletcher, R. 1957. *Instinct in Man*. New York: International Universities Press.

Flugel, J. C. 1921. *The Psychoanalytic Study of the Family*. London: Hogarth Press.

Ford, C., and Beach, F. A. 1951. *Patterns of Sexual Behavior*. New York: Harper.

Fortes, M. 1969. *Kinship and the Social Order*. Chicago: Aldine.

Foucault, M. 1965. *Madness and Civilization*. New York: Random House.

————. 1970. *The Order of Things*. New York: Random House.

Freeman, L. 1972. *The Story of Anna O*. New York: Walker.

Freud, A. 1965. *Normality and Pathology in Childhood: Assessment of Development*. In vol. 6 of *The Writings of Anna Freud*. New York: International Universities Press.

————. 1936. *The Ego and the Mechanisms of Defense*. New York: International Universities Press, 1946.

————, and Dann, S. 1951. An Experiment in Group Upbringing. *PSC* 6:127-68.

Freud, S. 1953-1974. *The Standard Edition of the Complete Psychological Works of Sigmund Freud*. London: Hogarth Press and Institute of Psychoanalysis. 24 volumes. All references to Freud are to the Standard Edition (SE).

Friedman, N. 1967. *The Social Nature of Psychological Research: The Psychological Experiment as a Social Interaction*. New York: Basic Books.

Fries, M. Psychosomatic Relationships between Mother and Infant. *PSM* 6:159-62.

Fromm, E. 1941. *Escape from Freedom*. New York: Farrar & Rinehart.

————. 1956. *The Art of Loving*. New York: Harper & Row.

————. 1973. *The Anatomy of Human Destructiveness*. New York: Norton.

————, and Maccoby, M. 1970. *Social Character in a Mexican Village*. Englewood Cliffs, N.J.: Prentice-Hall.

Furst, P., ed. 1972. *The Flesh of the Gods*. New York: Praeger.

Galbraith, J. K. 1967. *The New Industrial State*. Boston: Houghton Mifflin.

————. 1973. *Economics and the Public Purpose*. Boston: Houghton Mifflin.

Gilbert, F. 1971. The Historian and the World of the Twentieth Century: Post Scriptum. *Daedalus*, Spring, pp. 520-30.

Giovacchini, P. 1972. *Tactics and Techniques in Psychoanalytic Therapy*. Vol. 1. New York: Jason Aronson.

Goode, W. 1959. The Sociology of the Family. In *Sociology Today*, ed. R. Merton, L. Broom, and L. Cottrell, pp. 178-96. New York: Basic Books.

Goodenough, F. L. 1931. *Anger in Young Children*. Minneapolis: University of Minnesota Press.

Gould, R. 1972. *Child Studies Through Fantasy*. New York: Quadrangle Books.

Gouldner, A. 1972. *The Coming Crisis of Western Sociology*. New York: Basic Books.

Greenberg, J. 1963. *Universals of Language*. Cambridge: M.I.T. Press.

Greenblatt, D., and Shader, R. 1971. Meprobamate: A Study of Irrational Drug Use. *Amer. J. Psychiat.* 127:1297-1303.

Greenblatt, M. 1974. Psychopolitics. *Amer. J. Psychiat.* 131:1197-1203.

Greenson, R. R. 1962. On Enthusiasm. *JAPA* 10:3-21.

Greenstein, F. I. 1969. *Personality and Politics*. Chicago: Markham.

Greenwald, H. 1970. *The Elegant Prostitute.* New York: Walker.

Group for the Advancement of Psychiatry. 1966. *Psychiatry and Public Affairs.* Chicago: Aldine.

————. 1973. *The VIP with Psychiatric Impairment.* New York: Scribner.

Gunderson, J. G. (reporter). 1974. The Influence of Theoretical Model of Schizophrenia on Treatment Practice. *JAPA* 22:182-99.

Guntrip, H. 1961. *Personality Structure and Human Interaction.* New York: International Universities Press.

Gutheil, E. 1951. *The Handbook of Dream Analysis.* New York: Washington Square Press.

Hacker, F. 1972. Sublimation Revisited. *IJP* 53:219-23.

Hamburg, D. 1973. An Evolutionary and Developmental Approach to Human Aggressiveness. *PQ* 42:185-96.

————. et al. 1967. Report of Ad Hoc Committee on Central Fact-Gathering Data of the American Psychoanalytic Association. *JAPA* 15:841-61.

Handel, G. 1967. *The Psychosocial Interior of the Family.* Chicago: Aldine.

Hanson, N. R. 1965. *Patterns of Discovery.* Cambridge: Cambridge University Press.

Harlow, H. F. 1974. *Learning to Love.* New York: Jason Aronson.

Harris, F. R. 1970. *Social Science and National Policy.* Chicago: Aldine.

Harris, M. 1968. *The Rise of Anthropological Theory.* New York: Crowell.

Hartmann, E., ed. 1970. *Sleep and Dreaming.* Boston: Little, Brown.

————. 1973. *The Functions of Sleep.* New Haven: Yale University Press.

Hartmann, H. 1939. *Ego Psychology and the Problem of Adaptation.* New York: International Universities Press.

————. 1964. *Essays on Ego Psychology.* New York: International Universities Press.

————, Kris, E., and Lowenstein, R. M. 1946. Comments on the Formation of Psychic Structure. *PSC* 2:11-38.

Hauser, A. 1951. *The Social History of Art.* New York: Knopf.

Heilbroner, R. L. 1953. *The Worldly Philosophers.* New York: Simon & Schuster.

Heilbrun, A. B. 1973. *Aversive Maternal Control.* New York: Wiley.

Herzberg, F. 1966. *Work and the Nature of Man.* New York: World.

————, Mausner, B., and Snyderman, B. 1959. *The Motivation to Work.* New York: Wiley.

Hilgard, E. R. 1965. *Hypnotic Susceptibility.* New York: Harcourt, Brace & World.

Hofstadter, R. 1970. *American Violence.* New York: Knopf.

Hollingshead, A. B. 1949. *Elmtown's Youth.* New York: Wiley.

———— and Redlich, F. C. 1958. *Social Class and Mental Illness.* New York: Wiley.

Holt, R.; Klein, G.; Goldberger, L.; Barr, H.; and Langs, R. 1972. *LSD: Personality and Experience.* New York: Wiley.

Horney, K. 1937. *The Neurotic Personality of Our Time.* New York: Norton.

Hull, C. 1943. *Principles of Behavior.* New York: Appleton-Century-Crofts.

Hunt, M. 1959. *The Natural History of Love.* New York: Knopf.

Huxley, A. 1954. *The Doors of Perception.* New York: Harper.

Hymes, D., ed. 1969. *Reinventing Anthropology.* New York: Random House.

Israel, J., and Tajfel, H. 1972. *The Context of Social Psychology.* New York. Academic Press.

Jacobson, E. 1954. The Self and the Object World: Vicissitudes of Their Infantile Cathexes and Their Influence on Ideational and Affective Development. *PSC* 9:75-127.

————. 1959. Depersonalization. *JAPA* 7:581-610.

————. 1964. *The Self and the Object World,* New York: International Universities Press.

―――. 1971. *Depression*. New York: International Universities Press.

Janis, L. 1958. *Psychological Stress*. New York: Wiley.¹

Jelliffe, D. B., and Jelliffe, E. F. P., eds. 1971 The Uniqueness of Human Milk. *Amer. J. Clin. Nutrition*.

Jencks, C. 1972. *Inequality*. New York: Basic Books.

Jones, E. 1916. The Theory of Symbolism. In *Papers on Psychoanalysis*, pp. 87-144. London: Bailliere, Tyndall & Cox, 1948.

―――. 1918. Anal-Erotic Character Traits. In *Papers on Psychoanalysis*, 1948, pp. 413-37.

―――. 1924. Mother-Right and the Sexual Ignorance of Savages. In *Essays in Applied Psychoanalysis*, 1951, 2:145-73.

―――. 1929. Psychoanalysis and Psychiatry. In *Papers on Psychoanalysis*, 1948, pp. 365-78.

―――― 1957. *The Life and Work of Sigmund Freud*, 3 vols. New York: Basic Books.

Jung, C. G. 1964. *Man and His Symbols*. New York: Doubleday.

Kagan, J. 1971. *Change and Continuity in Infancy*. New York: Wiley.

Kahana, R., and Levin, S., eds. 1967. *Psychodynamic Studies on Aging: Creativity, and Dying*. New York: International Universities Press.

Kamiya, J. 1971. Preface in *Biofeedback and Self-Control*, ed. T. Barber et al. Chicago: Aldine-Atherton, 1971.

Kaplan, A. 1961. *The New World of Philosophies*. New York: Random House.

Kaplan, H., and Freedman, A. M., eds. 1967. *Comprehensive Textbook of Psychiatry*. Baltimore: Williams & Milkins.

Kardiner, A. 1939. *The Individual and His Society*. New York: Columbia University Press.

―――. 1945. *The Psychological Frontiers of Society*. New York: Columbia University Press.

Kaufman, W. 1971. Introduction in *Alienation*, ed. R. Schacht. New York: Doubleday.

Kern, S. 1974. The Onset of Bourgeois Sexual Morality. *Book Forum* 1:164-71.

Kernberg, O. A., et al. 1972. Psychotherapy and Psychoanalysis: Final Report. *Bull. Menninger Clinic* 36 (nos. 1-2).

―――. 1974. Barriers to Falling and Remaining in Love. *JAPA* 22:486-511.

Kety, S. S. 1958. Biochemical Theories of Schizophrenia. *Science* 129:1528-32, 1590-96.

Kiell, N. 1964. *The Universal Experience of Adolescence*. New York: International Universities Press.

Kiev, A., ed. 1964. *Magic, Faith, and Healing*. New York: Free Press.

Kimble, G. 1973. Scientific Psychology in Transition. In *Contemporary Approaches to Conditioning and Learning*, ed. F. McGuigan and D. B. Lumsden. Washington, D. C.: V. H. Winston.

Kinsey, A. C., et al. 1948. *Sexual Behavior in the Human Male*. Philadelphia: Saunders.

―――― et al. 1953. *Sexual Behavior in the Human Female*. Philadelphia: Saunders.

Klein, G. S., et al. 1959. Consciousness in Psychoanalytic Theory: Some Implications for Current Research in Perception. *JAPA* 7:5-34.

Klein, M. 1957. *Envy and Gratitude*. New York: Basic Books.

―――; Heimann, P.; Isaacs, S.; and Riviere, J. 1952. *Developments in Psychoanalysis*. London: Hogarth Press.

Kluckhohn, C. 1960. Recurrent Themes in Myths and Mythmaking. In *Myth and Mythmaking*, ed. H. Murray, pp. 46-60. New York: Braziller.

Knapp, R. H. 1956. Demographic, Cultural, and Personality Attributes of Scientists. In *Research Conference on the Identification of Creative Scientific*

Talent, ed. C. W. Taylor, pp. 204-212. Salt Lake City: University of Utah Press.

Koella, W. P. 1967. *Sleep: Its Nature and Physiological Organization.* Springfield, Ill.: Charles C Thomas.

Kohlberg, L.; La Crosse, J.; and Ricks, D. 1972. The Predictability of Adult Mental Health from Childhood Behavior. In *Manual of Child Psychopathology,* ed. B. Wolman, pp. 1217-84. New York: McGraw-Hill.

Kohut, H. 1971. *The Analysis of the Self.* New York: International Universities Press.

Komarovsky, M. 1962. *Blue-Collar Marriage.* New York: Random House.

Kornhauser, A. 1965. *Mental Health of the Industrial Worker.* New York: Wiley.

Kraepelin, E. 1917. *One Hundred Years of Psychiatry.* New York: Citadel Press, 1962.

Kramer, H., and Sprenger, J. 1486. *Malleus Maleficaruan.* London: Rodker, 1928.

Kris, E. 1952.*Psychoanalytic Explorations in Art.* New York: International Universities Press.

———. 1956. The Recovery of Childhood Memories in Psychoanalysis. *PSC* 1: 54-88.

———; Herma, J.; and Shor, J. 1943. Freud's Theory of the Dream in American Textbooks. *Abnorm. and Soc. Psych.* 30:319-34.

Kroeber, A. and Kluckhohn, C. 1952. *Culture.* New York: Random House.

Kuhn, T. 1962. *The Structure of Scientific Revolutions.* Chicago: University of Chicago Press.

Laffal, J. 1965. *Pathological and Normal Language.* New York: Atherton Press.

Laing, R. D. 1967. *The Politics of Experience.* New York: Ballantine Books.

Laslett, P., ed. 1972. *Household and Family in Past Time.* Cambridge: Cambridge University Press.

Lasswell, H. 1930. *Psychopathology and Politics.* New York: Viking Press, 1960.

Lawick-Goodall, J. van. 1973. The Behavior of Chimpanzees in Their Natural Habitat. *Amer. J. Psychiat.* 130:1-11.

Lehman, E. 1949. Feeding Problems of Psychogenic Origin. *PSC* 4:461-88.

Leighton, Alexander. 1959. *My Name Is Legion.* New York: Basic Books.

———. 1960. *People of Cove and Woodlot.* New York: Basic Books.

———. 1963. *The Character of Danger.* New York: Basic Books.

Levine, R. 1973. *Culture, Behavior, and Personality.* Chicago: Aldine.

Levy, D. M. 1943. *Maternal Overprotection.* New York: Columbia University Press.

Lewin, B. 1950. *The Psychoanalysis of Elation.* New York: Norton.

Lewis, H. 1970. The Royal Road to the Unconscious: Changing Conceptualizations of the Dream. In *Sleep and Dreaming,* ed. E. Hartmann, pp. 199-212. Boston: Littie, Brown.

———. 1971. *Shame and Guilt in Neurosis.* New York: International Universities Press.

Lewis, O. 1959. *Five Families.* New York: Basic Books.

Licht, H. 1932. *Sexual Life in Ancient Greece.* London: Abbey Library.

Lichtenstein, H. 1970. Changing Implications of the Concept of Psychosexual Development. *JAPA* 18:300-18.

Lidz, T. 1973. *The Origin and Treatment of Schizophrenic Disorders.* New York: Basic Books.

Lin Yutang. 1937. *The Importance of Living.* New York: Reynal & Hitchcock.

Lorenz, K. 1963. *On Aggression.* New York: Harcourt, Brace & World.

Luce, G. G. 1971. *Body Time.* New York: Random House.

Ludwig, A. 1965. *The Importance of Lying.* Springfield, Ill.: Charles C Thomas.

McCarthy, J., and McCarthy, J. 1969. *Learning Disabilities.* Boston: Allyn & Bacon.

McClelland, D. C. 1961. *The Achieving Society.* Princeton, N. J.: Van Nostrand.

McGill, V. F. 1967. *The Idea of Happiness.* New York: Praeger.

McGuigan, F. J., and Lumsden, D. B. 1973. *Contemporary Approaches to Conditioning and Learning.* Washington, D. C.: Winston.

Madow, L., and Snow, L. H., eds. 1970. *The Psychodynamic Implications of Physiological Studies on Sensory Deprivation.* Springfield, Ill.: Charles C Thomas.

Mahler, M. 1968. *On Human Symbiosis and the Vicissitudes of Individuation.* New York: International Universities Press.

Malinowski, M. 1923. Psycho-Analysis and Anthropology. *Psyche* 4:293-322.

————. 1963. Marriage. *Encyclopedia Britannica* 14:940-50.

Marshall, D., and Suggs, R., eds. 1971. *Human Sexual Behavior.* New York: Basic Books.

Mason, J. W. 1968. Organization of Psychoendocrine Mechanisms. *PSM* 30:565-808.

Masserman, J. H., ed. 1972. *The Dynamics of Power.* New York: Grune & Stratton.

Masters, W., and Johnson, V. 1966. *Human Sexual Response.* Boston: Little, Brown.

Mead, M. 1928. *Coming of Age in Samoa.* New York: Dell, 1967.

————. 1935. *Sex and Temperament in Three Primitive Societies.* New York: New American Library.

————. 1937. Interpretive Statement. In *Cooperation and Competition Among Primitive Peoples,* pp. 548-11. Boston: Beacon Press, 1961.

Medvedev, Z. 1971. *A Question of Madness.* New York: Vintage Books.

Meissner, W. W. 1974. The Role of Imitative Social Learning in Identificatory Processes. *JAPA* 22:512-36.

Merton, R. K. 1962. Bureaucratic Structure and Personality. In *Work, Man, and Modern Society,* ed. S. Nosow and W. Form, pp. 457-60. New York: Basic Books.

Minuchin, S., et al. 1967. *Families of the Slums,* New York: Basic Books.

Mitford, J. 1963. *The American Way of Death.* New York: Simon & Schuster.

Mitscherlich, A. 1971. Psychoanalysis and the Aggression of Large Groups. *IJP* 52:161-68.

Mittelmann, B., 1954. Motility in Infants, Children, and Adults. *PSC* 9:142-77.

Moriarty, A. E. 1966. *Constancy and I.Q. Change.* Springfield, Ill.: Charles C Thomas.

Mowrer, O. H. 1960. *Learning Theory and Behavior.* New York: Wiley.

Murdock, G. P. 1949. *Social Structure.* New York: Macmillan.

Murphy, G. 1972. *Historical Introduction to Modern Psychology.* New York: Harcourt Brace.

Myers, J., and Bean, L. L. 1968. *A Decade Later.* New York: Wiley.

National Commission on the Causes and Prevention of Violence. 1969. *The History of Violence in America.* New York: Bantam Books.

National Council on Family Relations. 1972. *Non-traditional Family Forms in the 1970's.* Minneapolis.

Neubauer, P. B. 1960. The One-Parent Child and His Oedipal Development. *PSC* 15:286-309.

Nordhoff, C. 1875. *The Communistic Societies of the United States.* New York: Schocken Books, 1965.

Norman, D. 1970. *Models of Human Memory.* New York: Academic Press.

Noy, P. 1969. A Revision of the Psychoanalytic Theory of the Primary Process. *IJP* 50:155-78.

Nunberg, H. 1955. *Principles of Psychoanalysis.* New York: International Universities Press.

Opler, M. K., ed. 1959. *Culture and Mental Health.* New York: Macmillan.

Palmore, E. 1969. Predicting Longevity. *Gerontology,* Winter.

Parkes, C. M. 1972. *Bereavement.* New York: International Universities Press.

Parkes, H. B. 1970. *The Divine Order.* London: Victor Gollanz.

Parsons, T. 1951. *The Social System.* Glencoe, Ill.: Free Press.

――― and Bales, R. 1955. *Family Socialization and Interaction Process.* Glencoe, Ill.: Free Press.

――― and Shils, E., eds. 1951. *Toward a General Theory of Action.* Cambridge: Harvard University Press.

Pettigrew, T. F. 1964. *A Profile of the Negro American.* Princeton, N. J.: Van Nostrand.

Pfister, O. 1944. *Christianity and Fear.* London: Allen & Unwin, 1948.

Phillips, D. L. 1973. *Abandoning Method.* San Francisco: Jossey-Bass.

Piaget, J. 1973. The Affective Unconscious and the Cognitive Unconscious. *JAPA* 21:249-61.

Post, S. C., ed. 1972. *Moral Values and the Superego Concept.* New York: International Universities Press.

Praz, M. 1951. *The Romantic Agony.* New York: World.

Provence, S., and Lipton, R. C. 1962. *Infants in Institutions.* New York: International Universities Press.

Rado, S. 1956. *Adaptational Psychodynamics.* New York: Jason Aronson, 1969.

Rangell, L. 1953. Psychiatric Aspects of Pain. *PSM* 15:22-37. .

Rank, O. 1909. *The Myth of the Birth of the Hero.* New York, Random House, 1932.

―――. 1932. *Art and the Artist.* New York: Tudor.

Rapaport, D. 1971. *Emotions and Memory.* New York: International Universities Press.

―――. 1960. The Structure of Psychoanalytic Theory. New York: InIternational Universities Press.

Redlich, F., and Freedman, D. 1966. *The Theory and Practice of Psychiatry.* New York: Basic Books.

Reich, W. 1927. *The Function of the Orgasm.* New York: Orgone Institute Press, 1942.

―――. 1933. *Character Analysis.* New York: Orgone Institute Press, 1949.

Reider, N. 1955. The Demonology of Modern Psychiatry. *Amer. J. Psychiat.* 11: 851-56.

Reik, T. 1951. *Masochism in Modern Man.* New York: Farrar, Strauss.

Rennie, T. A. C.; Srole, L.; Langer, T.; Michael, S.; and Opler, M. 1962. *Mental Health in the Metropolis: The Midtown Manhattan Study.* New York: McGraw-Hill.

Report from the Secretary of Health, Education and Welfare. 1973. *Alcohol and Health.* New York: Scribner.

Rheingold, H. L. 1963. *Maternal Behavior in Animals.* New York: Wiley.

Rheingold, J. 1967. *The Mother, Anxiety and Death.* Boston: Little, Brown.

Ricoeur, P. 1970. *Freud and Philosophy.* New Haven: Yale University Press.

Riesman, D., et al. 1961. *The Lonely Crowd.* New Haven: Yale University Press.

Roff, M., and Ricks, D., eds. 1969. *Life History Studies in Psychopathology.* Minneapolis: University of Minnesota Press.

Rogers, D., ed. 1969. *Issues in Adolescent Psychology.* New York: Appleton-Century-Crofts.

Róheim, G. 1932. Psycho-Analysis of Primitive Cultural Types. *IJP* 13:1-224.

―――. 1950. *Psychoanalysis and Anthropology.* New York: International Universities Press.

Rooth, A. G. 1957. Creation Myths. *Anthropos* 52:497-508.

Rosen, G. 1968. *Madness in Society*. New York: Harper & Row.

Rosen, J. 1953. *Direct Analysis*. New York: Grune & Stratton.

Rosenbaum, M. 1952. The Challenge of Group Psychoanalysis. *Psychoanalysis* 1: 50-58.

———— and Berger, M. 1975. *Group Psychotherapy and Group Function*. New York: Basic Books.

Rosenfeld, H. A. 1954. Considerations Regarding the Psycho-Analytic Approach to Acute and Chronic Schizophrenia. *IJP* 35:135-60.

Rosenhahn, D. L. 1973. On Being Sane in Insane Places. *Science* 179 (no. 4070): 250.

Rosenthal, R. 1966. *Experimenter Effects in Behavioral Research*. New York: Appleton-Century-Crofts.

Ross, N. 1970. The Primacy of Genitality in the Light of Ego Psychology: Introductory Remarks: *JAPA* 18:267-84.

Ruesch, J. 1972. *Disturbed Communication*. New York: Norton.

Sandler, J., and Joffe, W. G. 1969. Towards a Basic Psychoanalytic Model. *IJP* 50:79-90.

Saperstein, J., and Gaines, J. 1973. The Self. *IJP* 54:415-24.

Sapir, E. 1921. *Language*. New York: Harcourt, Brace.

Schafer, R. 1964. The Clinical Analysis of Affects. *JAPA* 12:275-99.

————. 1968. *Aspects of Internalization*. New York: International Universities Press.

————. 1973. Action: Its Place in Psychoanalytic Interpretation and Theory. In Chicago Institute of Psychoanalysis, *The Annual of Psychoanalysis*. New York: Quadrangle Books.

Schaller, G. B. 1965. *The Year of the Gorilla*. New York: Ballantine.

Schneider, D. 1950. *The Psychoanalyst and the Artist*. New York: International Universities Press.

Schur, M. 1955. Comments on the Metapsychology of Somatization. *PSC* 10:119-64.

————. 1966. *The Id and the Regulatory Principles of Mental Functioning*. New York: International Universities Press.

————. 1972. *Freud: Living and Dying*. New York: International Universities Press.

Sechehaye, M. A. 1956. *A New Psychotherapy in Schizophrenia: Relief of Frustrations by Symbolic Realization*. New York: Grune & Stratton.

Selye, Hans, 1956. *The Stress of Life*. New York: McGraw-Hill.

Sharpe, E. 1935. Similar and Divergent Unconscious Determinants Underlying the Sublimations of Pure Art and Pure Science. In *Collected Papers on Psychoanalysis*. London: Hogarth Press, 1950.

Sherman, G. 1969. Soviet Youth: Myth and Reality. In *Issues in Adolescent Psychology*, ed. D. Rogers, pp. 576-91.

Siegman, A. 1954. Emotionality: A Hysterical Character Defense. *PQ* 23:339-54.

Simirenko, A. 1969. *Social Thought in the Soviet Union*. Chicago: Quadrangle Books.

Singer, J. L. 1966. *Daydreaming*. New York: Random House.

Skinner, B. F. 1971. *Beyond Freedom and Dignity*. New York: Knopf.

Slovenko, R. 1973. *Psychiatry and Law*. Boston: Little, Brown.

Socarides, C. 1968. *The Overt Homosexual*. New York: Grune & Stratton.

Sorokin, P. 1941. *The Crisis of Our Age: The Social and Cultural Outlook*. New York: Dutton.

Spector, J. J. 1972. *The Aesthetics of Freud*. New York: Praeger.

Sperling, M. 1949. The Role of the Mother in Psychosomatic Disorders in Children. *PSM* 11:377.

Spiegel, L. 1954. Acting Out and Defensive Instinctual Gratification. *JAPA* 2: 117-19.

Spiegel, R. 1959. Specifific Problems of Communication. In *American Handbook of Psychiatry*, ed. S. Arieti, pp. 909-49. New York: Basic Books.

Spiro, M. and Burrows, E. 1957. *An Atoll Culture.* New Haven: Behavior Science Monographs.

Spitz, R. 1952. Authority and Masturbation: Some Remarks on a Bibliographical Investigation. *PQ* 21:490-527.

———. 1957. *No and Yes.* New York: International Universities Press.

———. 1965. *The First Year of Life.* New York: International Universities Press.

Stein, M. J.; Vidich, A. I.; and White, D. M., eds. 1960. *Identity and Anxiety.* Glencoe, Ill.: Free Press.

Sternbach, R. A. 1968. *Pain: A Psychophysiological Analysis.* New York: Academic Press.

Stoller, R. J. 1968. *Sex and Gender.* New York: Jason Aronson.

Stone, L. J., et al. 1973. *The Competent Infant.* New York: Basic Books.

Sullivan, H. S. 1924. *Schizophrenia as a Human Process.* New York: Norton, 1962.

———. 1940. *Conceptions of Modern Psychiatry.* New York: Norton.

———. 1964. *The Fusion of Psychiatry and Social Science.* New York: Norton.

Sumner, W. 1906. *Folkways.* New York: Dover, 1959.

Szasz, T. 1971. The Sane Slave: An Historical Note on the Use of Medical Diagnosis as Justificatory Rhetoric. In *Psychotherapy*, pp. 85-96. Chicago: Aldine.

———, ed. 1973. *The Age of Madness.* New York: Jason Aronson.

Tart, C. T., ed. 1969. *Altered States of Consciousness.* New York: Wiley.

Thrasher, F. 1926. *The Gang.* Chicago: University of Chicago Press.

Tinbergen, N. 1951. *The Study of Instinct.* Oxford: Clarendon Press.

Turnbull, C. M. 1972. *The Mountain People.* New York: Simon & Schuster.

U.S. News and World Report. 1973. The Pursuit of Happiness. August 27, pp. 34-40.

Varendonck, J. 1921. *The Psychology of Daydreams.* New York: Macmillan.

Waelder, R. 1960. *The Basic Theory of Psychoanalysis.* New York: International Universities Press.

Wallace, A. F. C. 1970. *Culture and Personality.* New York: Random House.

Ward, R. 1971. *The Living Clocks.* New York: Knopf.

Weber, M. 1904. *The Protestant Ethic and the Spirit of Capitalism.* New York: Scribner, 1958.

Weinberg, S. K. 1955. *Incest Behavior.* New York: Citadel Press.

Whiting, J., and Child, I. 1953. *Child Training and Personality.* New Haven: Yale University Press.

Whyte, W. H. 1956. *The Organization Man.* Garden City, N.Y.: Anchor Books, Doubleday.

Wickler, W. 1972. *The Sexual Code.* New York: Doubleday.

Wiener, N. 1953. *Ex-Prodigy: My Childhood and Youth.* Cambridge: M.I.T. Press.

Wise, D. 1973. *The Politics of Lying.* New York: Random House.

Witkin, H.; Lewis, H. B.; Hertzman, M.; Machover, M.; Meissner, P. B.; and Wapner, S. 1954. *Personality Through Perception.* New York: Harper.

Wolberg, A. 1973. *The Borderline Patient.* New York: Intercontinental Medical Books.

Wolfenstein, E. 1971. *Revolutionary Personalities: Lenin, Trotsky, Gandhi.* Princeton: Princeton University Press.

Wolff, H. G. 1968. *Stress and Disease,* 2nd ed. Springfield, Ill.: Charles C Thomas.

Work in America. Report of a Special Task Force to the Secretary of Health, Education and Welfare. Cambridge: M.I.T. Press, 1972.

Wynne, L. C. 1970. Communication Disorders and the Quest for Relatedness in Families of Schizophrenics. In R. Cancro, ed., *Annual Review of the Schizophrenic Syndrome,* vol. 2, 1972, pp. 395-414. New York: Brunner/Mazel.

Yablonsky, L. 1970. *The Violent Gang.* Baltimore: Penguin Books.

————. 1965. *Synanon: The Tunnel Back.* New York: Macmillan.

Yankelovich, D. 1972. *The Changing Values on Campus: Political and Personal Attitudes on Campus.* New York: Washington Square Press.

Zubek, J. P., ed. 1969. *Sensory Deprivation.* New York: Appleton-Century-Crofts.

Zwerling, I. 1955. The Favorite Joke in Diagnostic and Therapeutic Interviewing. *PQ* 24:104-14.

Index